STAYED

American GI's
Communist China —
and Why They Stayed

With a Prefatory Note by CARL SANDBURG

FARRAR, STRAUS AND CUDAHY | NEW YORK

Manufactured in the United States of America
by American Book–Stratford Press, Inc., New York

Published simultaneously in Canada
by Ambassador Books, Ltd., Toronto

To

ALICIA PATTERSON

who not only inspired this book

but made it possible for me to write it

January 7, 1955

Dear Alicia

Thank you for having tearsheets sent to me of Virginia Pasley's "Twenty-One Stayed." I have read many stories in this field but this one gets to the roots and branches more thoroughly than any I have read. I salute Virginia Pasley's endurance and intelligence, her keen human sympathies, her superb summation at the end. This has the proportions of a book, the documentary of a dark epic. There may have been another series of articles more deserving of a Pulitzer award but I have not met it. Seldom in past years has a Pulitzer award been made for an achievement of the proportion of "Twenty-One Stayed."

Ever good wishes

CARL SANDBURG

Contents

Contents

21 *STAYED*

Introduction

On JANUARY 23, 1954, twenty-one American youths, all but one brought up in American towns and rural communities, educated in American schools, all trained in an American army, turned their backs on family and friends, home and country to accept the philosophy and the way of life of the Chinese Reds who had held them in Korean prison camps for three years or more.

Though this country has had its Benedict Arnolds, never before has a group of American prisoners of war chosen to remain with their captors. Of more significance, never before has a group of Americans taken an active part in a propaganda campaign directed against their own country.

Why did they do it? Was there anything they had in common? Could a clue be found in their backgrounds, their early lives, their schooling? Was the army to blame? Or was it just fate and circumstances?

These were questions that Alicia Patterson, editor and publisher of the Long Island newspaper *Newsday*, and I were discussing that last week in January. We couldn't find the answers. The surveys that had been made in the months since it was known American soldiers planned to stay with the enemy gave little more than sketchy, inconclusive pictures.

"How would you like to go to all their home towns and see if you can find the answers?" Miss Patterson asked me.

1—

Of course I would.

So it was that I made my strange three-month tour up and down America by train and plane, bus, and rented car. I cannot recommend my itinerary to those looking for out-of-the-way spots, though many were, certainly, enough out of the way. There were unexpected brushes with beauty, but even spring could not give a luster to some of the places I visited.

I traveled more than fifteen thousand miles into twenty-three states. I went to the home towns of every one of the twenty-one, and if their families had moved, to the new home towns; to cities like Detroit and Providence and Baltimore, Memphis and Jacksonville; to hamlets barely on the map, Texon and Blooming Grove, West Fort Ann and East Carondelet; down dirt roads to farms in country about as far back as you can get.

I talked to families and friends, to neighbors and relatives, to storekeepers and employers, to teachers and preachers and welfare workers.

Everywhere I went I also talked to prisoners of war who did come back, ranging from a corporal who received the Bronze Star for his heroism in prison camp to a private first class who collaborated with the Chinese Reds and still thinks his country is wrong and the twenty-one who stayed are heroes.

I got doors slammed in my face and I got unexpected cooperation in unlikely places. There were some who wouldn't talk and there were some who couldn't talk.

I found that slums in a country town can be every bit as dismal as those in a city; that when the land is unkind, poverty is doubly bleak, with neighbors few and far between.

I found a curious contradiction: Americans are always on the move, particularly doctors, ministers, teachers and the young; but Americans are stay-at-homes—ring someone's bell and the chances are good he'll answer it. I was lucky, too. I drove one hundred fifty miles to see the mother of one boy and caught her just as she was about to leave on a two weeks' journey.

In the face of tragedy people can be kind; most were eager to understand rather than to condemn. Of all the groups I talked to the teachers stand out. From the four-room schoolhouse to the new million dollar high school, they seldom forgot a child they had ever taught, even though he was a "quiet one." They understand their pupils better than do the parents. Above all else, they have an amazing humility and sense of responsibility. Over and over, from coast to coast, teachers would say, "We failed with that boy," or "We should have done more to help him."

Tracing some of the families and the backgrounds of some of the boys became as involved as a detective story. It took an all-day tour of the parish houses of a large town to find out where one boy had spent his early years. It took three days to trace one boy's mother only to find her in a hospital.

The married name of one boy's aunt—the only one left who knew his story—turned up by a fluke. A three-hundred-mile trip was necessary to discover that the information I wanted on another was to be had right where I had started.

Many had moved four or five times in their short lives before they went into the army and had to be trailed from neighborhood to neighborhood, school to school. While most were well remembered by some few at least, there were two or three who seemed not to have made a dent in anyone's life.

I seldom knew one day where I would be the next, for one clue led to another somewhere else and my itinerary was revised as often as it was made up.

I had a flashbulb camera with me—called foolproof—which frightened more people than it photographed. So it stayed in the car most of the time. Of the photographs that turned out at all *Newsday*'s art editor, trying for kind words, said they had "the immediacy of pictures taken under war conditions."

There were the strange airports and the strange rented cars and the almost missed planes and the rush to get through with the schools on Friday so that there would be no weekend waits. There were the good hotels and the bad ones including the one in southern Illinois and the room that had just been painted—the half empty pails were still there. There were the motels with television sets rentable at a quarter an hour that would go blank in the middle of a program with no more quarters available.

There were dust storms in Texas, rain in California and atomic snowfall in Minnesota. There were the fantastic country directions: "Go down the highway about a mile, then take the left road, the left fork that is, go up the road a piece—you cross three bridges (planks, that is) then turn right; at the next four corners turn left, then follow the road keeping left and you can't miss it, the green house with the broken shutters." And of course you missed it and came back to the starting point and tried all over, or asked someone else and got an even more elaborate set of directions.

There was the suitcase in one hand that got heavier and heavier with papers until there was room for only one change of clothes, and the typewriter in the other and the race without benefit of porter up the stairs to a train for Altoona that would have been missed except that the Cleveland Indians were taking it and Bob Lemon couldn't be found.

This was only the frame, sometimes light and sometimes dim, for what was essentially a somber picture. The towns I toured and the homes I visited had been hit by tragedy harder to bear and understand than death itself, made more exquisite because hope, however forlorn, was still possible. Yet long before the last doorbell was rung, the pattern had emerged, the hows and the whys were answered.

The Korean War

THE KOREAN WAR was the most curious war in history. It was three wars, depending on how you looked at it: a simple civil war between two parts of a divided country; the first widespread attempt at collective resistance by the United Nations to an aggressor; or a hot offshoot of the Cold War between the United States and the Soviet Union. Half of its three-year length was fought to defend a principle which, it turned out, would make it possible for twenty-one American youths to give up their country and stay with the enemy.

Never has this country entered a war with such high hopes and ended it with such irritable disillusion. The initial unanimity which backed the United Nations decision to fight against aggression and the United States decision to send in its troops faded swiftly when it turned out that American troops would actually have to fight and die in Korea.

When the early defeats were repeated because of the intervention of the Chinese Communists, after victory seemed assured, and the war settled down to a long dreary bloody stalemate near the 38th parallel, Americans became divided.

Some wanted our forces to carry the war home to the Chinese Reds and at least bomb their bases. Some wanted peace at any price. Most didn't know quite what they wanted except that they were weary of a war which didn't get any place, was being fought in a country they had heard of only recently, with impossible names and improbable customs, and for a reason they had forgotten if they ever knew it.

The basis for the struggle was laid when, Japan out of the war, American and Soviet troops raced to be the first to "liberate" its long-time satellite state, Korea, that sore thumb peninsula of the continent of Asia.

The two forces met roughly at the 38th parallel and the division of the country into two parts, one under Soviet sponsorship and the other under American, was the result. The United States made South Korea a ward of the United Nations. The Russians refused to do the same for North Korea and sought to annex the southern sector by one means or another.

On the morning of June 25, 1950, nearly 100,000 North Korean troops broke over the 38th parallel to attack South Korea, claiming retaliation for border incidents.

It was Sunday morning and the radio was carrying the news of the invasion and the fact that the Security Council had been called into emergency session. My husband, Fred D. Pasley, was covering the United Nations for the New York *Daily News*. We raced to Lake Success, then the U.N. headquarters.

I will not easily forget the atmosphere in which the Council debated that day. Everyone there knew that if the Security Council compromised on this, the United Nations was finished and its hope for peace in the world was gone. At the end of four hours of consideration, the Council called on the North Koreans to "cease fire" and on all member nations to aid the U.N. and "refrain from giving assistance to the North Koreans."

On Monday, President Truman gave orders to the navy and air force to support South Korea. One Tuesday the U.N. Security Council met again, ordered military sanctions against the North Koreans and asked all member nations to aid in the fight for South Korea. Optimism ran high. The speedy action, the call for military force, would convince the North Koreans—and the Russians—that their invasion was a mistake. The war would be stopped before it started.

The optimism was premature. The Soviets had walked out of the Security Council early that month and continued their boycott of it throughout these crucial sessions. Had they attended, their veto power could have kept the Security Council from taking any action. Why they didn't is still an unresolved mystery.

Having missed that chance, they now took the position that the Security Council's action was illegal because neither the Russians nor the Chinese Communists were represented on it. The war went on.

United States troops were started to Korea within a week; 1,000 men from the 24th Division were flown in on July 1. Others came by transport until there were six divisions committed by the middle of September. By that time the green South Korean troops and the small detachments of Americans had been beaten back to a beachhead around Pusan on the west coast of Korea.

But the final divisions were brought in by a daring invasion landing at Inchon farther to the north. The beachhead was swiftly enlarged and the North Koreans were pushed back to the 38th parallel in less than two weeks.

On October 1, General MacArthur called on the North Korean government to surrender. On October 7, he sent United Nations troops across the 38th parallel on a race up to the Yalu River border between North Korea and Manchuria. Already there had been rumors of Chinese "volunteers" fighting with the North Koreans. Communist China's Premier, Chou En-lai, gave a radio warning that the Chinese would not "stand idly by" while the territory of their neighbor was invaded by "imperialists."

These portents were brushed aside as United Nations troops still in summer uniform drove on to capture the North Korean capital of Pyongyang and to go on to the Yalu River. Tens of thousands of North Korean soldiers surrendered. MacArthur estimated that only 40,000 were left to fight.

South Korean regiments were the first to know that the Chinese Communists had entered the war in earnest late in October. The American First Cavalry met their burp guns a few days later on Hallowe'en. On November 6, MacArthur announced that "a new and fresh army now faces us." Still, troops on other parts of the front continued their drive to the Yalu. The Chinese were conducting a hit-and-run war and the possibility that they were token forces or merely protecting their border was not yet dismissed.

On November 21 the 7th Division reached Hyesanjin on the Yalu River and planted the American flag on its banks. Peace rumors spread. Winter supplies began to catch up with the troops, including turkeys for Thanksgiving dinner. On November 24, MacArthur ordered the offensive that was to end the war. By the evening of the 25th the Chinese Communists had marshalled for a counteroffensive that shattered the U.N. forces all across the front before the lull came on December 2. More than half of the twenty-one who stayed were captured during this period.

Retreat was as swift as the victory march. Instead of being home by Christmas the soldiers were back at the 38th parallel with a new and stronger enemy fronting them.

During the next few months a series of fierce attacks were made by both sides. The U.N. forces were pushed back behind the 38th parallel and the South Korean capital of Seoul was taken and retaken, but the lines held generally firm. The United Nations took notice of the new entrant in the war and named Communist China as an aggressor in February of 1951.

In April, President Truman recalled General MacArthur, who had been Commander not only of United States forces but of the United Nations forces as well, after he openly criticized Administration policies and protested not being given authority to bomb Communist bases in China or use Nationalist troops from Formosa.

The war went on. Late in May the Chinese attacked in a massive spring offensive. Casualties mounted. But by June the 38th parallel and the initiative were in the possession of the U.N. forces.

Most members of the United Nations felt that the mission of their forces had been accomplished: the invader had been driven out of South Korea. The Communists on their part recognized that they had lost the opportunity to push the U.N. troops into the sea. It was time to talk of peace.

Truce talks began on July 10, 1951, and bogged down immediately over the question of what would be discussed. Even the meeting place was a subject for dissension until Panmunjom, a mud hut village off the east coast and not far from the 38th parallel, was chosen.

During the next two years meetings were held intermittently, sometimes every day, sometimes after a lapse of weeks or months.

By the end of 1951, agreement of a sort had been reached or seemed possible on every major point except the question of prisoners of war and their repatriation. Thousands of Chinese and North Korean troops captured during the fighting had asked political asylum. Some had deserted to escape Communism. The United States, as a matter of principle, had declared that it would not force any war prisoner who did not wish it to go back to the Reds.

The Chinese, on their part, insisted that every prisoner on the list must be returned to them, forcibly if necessary. Neither side would back down and the war went on for another year and a half with occasional truce talks and occasional battles, neither accomplishing anything, except that more soldiers were killed, wounded and captured.

By this time the Korean war was not only unpopular; to many Americans—and to Canadians, too, who had a brigade at the front—it had become dull and uninteresting. A Vancouver newspaper repeated the same dispatch from the front lines of Korea for three days running, using even the same headline. Not one single reader called to complain. Even the editorial staff of the paper itself—except for one man—failed to notice it.

This apathy was contagious enough to be caught not only by prisoners of war but by the soldiers at the front who felt cut off from the world anyway. The stalemate situation which continued to the end of the war did not help their morale.

Not only returned prisoners of war but even soldiers who had never spent time in prison camps were hazy about why they had been in Korea in the first place and what the war was all about.

Then in March of 1953 Stalin died and Malenkov became Premier. Three weeks later the Chinese proposed a resumption of the peace negotiations which had been at a standstill for weeks, announcing they would agree to an immediate exchange of sick and wounded prisoners.

Operation "Little Switch," as it was known, began in April. A little more than 600 Allied prisoners were returned in exchange for more than 6,000 Chinese and North Koreans.

Many of the prisoners of war who came back then had neither been wounded or sick, but were supposedly staunch "progressives," as prisoners who had cooperated with their Chinese jailers were called.

The peace meetings were resumed on April 27 and by early June the armistice agreement was almost ready for signing. Syngman Rhee, the fiery old president of the South Korean republic, had been practically ignored in the final negotiations.

When he discovered that the agreement would include an opportunity for Communist teams to interview prisoners of war who refused repatriation, he ordered the prison camps under his control opened to protect the recalcitrant North Koreans from Communist "brainwashing."

On June 18, more than 24,000 of the 35,000 North Koreans who had refused to return to Communist domination were led out of their camps and spirited away to the hills where they were given clothes and resident cards.

The measure of how much the Chinese wanted the war to end was shown when this incident delayed but did not end the armistice negotiations. The last detail was ironed out and the agreement signed on July 27. Ten hours later the guns were quieted and the war was over.

The complicated prisoner exchange was to take another six months. U.N. commanders had been shocked when, on exchange of prisoner of war lists back in December of 1951, they found that the Communists had named less than 12,000 Allied prisoners as against their official claims of having captured 65,000. More than 10,000 Americans were missing at that time and the Communist list accounted for less than a third of these. The proportion of South Koreans was even smaller. The year and a half of stalemate war had added few prisoners to the lists on either side and the proportion remained about the same when the exchange started. On September 3, the last batches of prisoners of war willing to go home had been exchanged.

Under the agreement, prisoners of war who refused repatriation were to be given into the custody of a Neutral Nations Repatriation Commission, including India, which had agreed to furnish the troops needed to guard them.

Communist reporters at Panmunjom had already leaked the news that a number of Americans would refuse to return home. When the Commission took custody the names of twenty-three were announced. In addition 325 South Koreans had cast their lot with the Communists.

On the other side there were 23,000 Chinese and North Koreans, besides the thousands Syngman Rhee had freed, who refused to go back to their homes.

The agreement provided that the Indians were to hold both groups for ninety days while explaining teams from the prisoners' own countries were to have a chance to convince them they should return. After another thirty-day grace period they were to be turned loose as "civilians" and assisted in getting to a neutral country.

Many of the North Koreans and Chinese refused to meet with the Communist "explainers." Few of those who listened were moved. Out of the 23,000, 765 changed their minds and went back home.

The Americans also refused to meet with the repatriation teams and when loudspeakers were tuned into their compound whooped it up so that the pleas could not be heard. Nevertheless, in October, during the ninety-day explaining period, one prisoner of war asked the Indian guard to let him out—he was Cpl. Edward S. Dickenson of Cracker's Neck, Va. Just before the end of the final thirty days' grace, Cpl.

13—

Claude Batchelor of Kermit, Tex. managed to escape the surveillance of the group and left the compound. Dickenson was court-martialed and has appealed his ten-year sentence. Batchelor was court-martialed and is serving a twenty-year sentence.

When January 23, 1954—the final deadline—came, there were still twenty-one American prisoners of war who had not openly wavered in their decision to stay with the Communists. Five days later they went behind the Iron Curtain.

The Twenty-One

W<small>HAT ARE THEY LIKE</small>, these twenty-one who could have come back to home and country, who had a stake of $5,000 waiting for them in back pay to give them a new start, who chose instead to stay with the Communists?

On the surface they seem like any other group of American youths. On the surface they aren't any different than the kid down the street. Some are tall and some are short. Some have blue eyes and some have brown; some are bright and some are dull.

Three are Negroes, the rest white. Sixteen are Protestants of various denominations; four are Roman Catholics; one is a Greek Catholic; there are no Jews.

All but one are native-born. All but one had native-born parents. They come from north and south, east and west, seventeen different states and one foreign country, Belgium. Only one comes from a really big metropolitan city.

Take twenty-one out of one hundred sixty million Americans and it won't even ruffle a statistic. Take twenty-one out of 2,500,000 soldiers and it will barely move a decimal point. Take twenty-one out of four thousand surviving prisoners of war and you still have only one half of one per cent. Not many, statistically speaking. But these twenty-one are not statistics. They are living, breathing American youths, who once roamed the piney woods of southern Louisiana, hunted over the foothills of New York's Adirondacks, swam in the lazy waters of Florida or the bracing surf of California—and will no more.

These are boys who grew up in Ohio, Texas and Pennsylvania, Minnesota and Mississippi, Rhode Island, Oklahoma, Tennessee and Illinois, Arkansas, Michigan, Georgia and Maryland—and have exchanged their homelands for the alien vistas of Communist-dominated China.

Why did they do it? There is no single answer; there are no easy answers.

Some of the answers are implicit in the stories of their lives. Some are found in the story of what happened to the American G.I. who was taken prisoner by the Reds. One essential difference between the kid down the street and the twenty-one is that he wasn't put into the front lines in Korea and didn't spend three years in prison camp.

The biggest haul of American prisoners the Reds got was in the fateful winter of 1950-51. Most of the twenty-one were captured then; ten of them in one forty-eight-hour period— November 30, December 1.

This was the time of the scandal over lack of ammunition, winter clothing and other supplies for our front line troops. It was also the time when they first came up against the Chinese hordes.

"Our Intelligence had broken down," a returned prisoner of war who accepted the line he was given in prison camp told me. "They told us there were no Chinese in the area, and then we were slaughtered. It was a pitiful war."

He spoke bitterly of junior officers and noncoms who went back to safe positions and sent their orders up by radio, then contradicted that by telling how the captain of his company was captured with him.

That might be dismissed as a typical gripe of a disgruntled dogface, but all the prisoners of war agreed that the front was disorganized and confused; that supplies didn't reach them, whatever the reason; that they never knew what hit them until it was all over.

Prisoners were taken all along the front, but most of them were from the 2nd Division, the outfit that had been thrown into the line right after hostilities started and had carried the weight of the fighting in the five months since then.

The circumstances of capture varied and those circumstances had some effect on what happened to the prisoners later. Many were wounded. Few of these survived. Those who did survive were exposed to psychological as well as physical stresses such as American troops had never before undergone.

What was it like to be a prisoner of war in the control of the Chinese People's Voluntary Committee?

Here is what happened to a typical G.I. who did survive; call him Joe.

He was captured when the remnants of his company were surrounded by a Chinese force that wasn't supposed to be there. He had a small scratch on his arm. It was nothing; but later it became infected. He was suffering a little from battle shock. He hadn't eaten anything since the day before.

On the long miserable march up to the Yalu River where the prison camps were set up, Joe did what his sergeant told him to do. He took his turn at litter carrying, and slogged along the rest of the time. One or two in his company refused to accept the sergeant's authority any longer; one or two did more than they were asked to; both were in the minority.

When they got to camp at last, the top sergeants were culled out. Joe and his buddies were on their own so far as army discipline was concerned, so far as army leadership was concerned.

Joe saw a lot of friends and strangers die on the march north to the Manchurian border. They kept on dying those first few months in camp.

The food was barely edible, parched corn and gruel—"food for animals, not men." It didn't help the gnawing pains in Joe's stomach to note that the Chinese guards had little more. His weight went down from 160 to 110.

There were not enough doctors or even medical corpsmen to do much for the wounded. Medicines, even aspirin, were not to be had after their own supplies were exhausted. The scratch on Joe's arm festered but there was nothing to put on it.

Neither barracks life nor the restraints of the fighting front had been enough to prepare Joe for the tight confinement and complete lack of privacy of prison life. The overcrowding at the camp was so extreme that in some huts men could not lie down to sleep; there wasn't room for all to stretch out at once. Lice, dysentery, pneumonia, and later malaria spread through the camp, killing those already weakened and weakening those who up to then had kept their strength.

Joe's hut was heated with a wood stove, but there was never enough wood to do more than keep the temperature somewhat above freezing.

Loudspeakers blared Communist propaganda at them from morning to night. Joe was forced to attend lectures, study classes, monitored discussion groups.

At any hour of the day or night a guard might come in and give a new order or take one of his companions away without explanation. Some he never saw again. Some came back, weak and half frozen from days in solitary; some turned up in newly built huts with more elbowroom and better food.

—18

One of these last was Bill, an eighteen-year-old Pfc. from another platoon. Bill had been captured by a Chinese who could speak English and who had stretched out his hand to him saying:

"We come in peace; do not fear us."

Bill had then been singled out to be interrogated first. They asked him no military questions. He wouldn't have known any answers anyway. They were friendly and kind, he said. They asked him what an American boy was doing so far away from home fighting in a war that was none of his affair; meddling in a purely local, family affair.

Bill didn't have any answer to that. He had wondered himself. Joe couldn't enlighten him. He didn't know, either.

Now they took Bill up to headquarters. They reiterated what the loudspeakers had been droning incessantly, that this was an "American imperialist war," planned by Wall Street. They told him that it was Wall Street that had supplied him with "bazookas that wouldn't shoot and tanks that had the most important bolts missing." Bill bought that. They asked him to sign a peace petition. He signed it. That was when he was transferred to the new hut.

Meanwhile Joe and some of his buddies had gotten into trouble. They had been caught stealing food from the storage barn and they had been beaten for it even though all they'd found was more cracked corn. When they got hungry enough they tried it again. This time all but one was caught. That was Al. The rumor was soon current that Al had told on the gang. They gave him the silent treatment. The next time, Al did tell.

That incident was typical. Everything that went on in Joe's hut got to the ears of the Communists. Informers seemed to be everywhere. Some informed because they had swallowed the bait; some did it to get better food or medicine; some like Al because they had the name, why not the game; some because they had come to feel cornered for one reason or another. Joe began to feel there wasn't anyone he could trust.

In the summer of 1951, peace talks were started and life became slightly more bearable for the prisoners. The Communists now made some attempt at a semblance of conformance to the standards of the Geneva Convention. The food improved. There was more of it when the talks went well for the Communists; less whenever the negotiations were stalled.

Attendance at propaganda lectures and study groups was made "voluntary" but the pressures to keep on going were hard to resist. Some of his hutmates argued that you might as well "do what the man says" and save yourself trouble and some—the minority—were beginning to talk like they believed the stuff. About that time a newly captured corporal, Jim, joined their company and organized a secret study group of his own to combat Communist propaganda and present the other side. This wasn't easy. He had no books or newspapers to work with; no printed matter was allowed in camp unless it had a Marxist or Communist slant. There was no access to the true facts to counteract Communist-colored current news broadcasts.

This class wasn't secret very long. Jim was put in solitary —a hole in the ground, a dugout or root cellar. When he was let out, his hutmates massaged his frozen hands and feet back to life. Others broke under this treatment but Jim kept on with his attempts to counteract Communist propaganda until they pulled him out of the hut and sent him to a camp for "reactionaries," as the Communists termed those who wouldn't go along with them.

The minority who stayed with the study groups were, little by little, enticed into other activities. Some formed

Kremlin clubs for advanced study, some made propaganda recordings and wrote propaganda articles for the camp newspaper and Communist papers around the world. They wrote letters home, asking their parents to get into the peace movement, complaining about the war, and praising the good treatment they were getting from the Chinese Reds.

Some were given jobs, such as camp librarian, liaison man, mailman or mess committeeman. All got better food, better medical attention and had greater freedom of movement.

They called themselves "progressives" and, though many of the prisoners who stayed outside the group referred to them as "birdies" because they "sang," the name progressive or "Pro" has stuck. Still, only 10 per cent of the prisoners were in that classification. Eventually most of them were sent to Camp Number V to keep them from being ganged up on by the "reactionaries." To this camp also were sent candidates for "progressivism."

Among the candidates was a whole company of Negroes drawn from all the prison camps and put in an enclosure by themselves. The Communists had not had as much luck taking the Negroes "into camp" as they had expected and they thought they might do better if they appealed to them as a group. This time the Communists outsmarted themselves and the plan backfired.

"They told us there was no segregation in Communist countries," returned Negroes reported, "and then they segregated us.

"Besides, a lot of our boys had been worked over by the Communists at home. They knew the answers and they gave most of the rest of us the benefit of their experience."

The pressure to sign peace petitions never let up. They worked on everyone, "progressives," "reactionaries" and the unclassified.

For some who had gone along just for the ride, for others who felt lingering doubts that what the Communists were telling them was true, the clincher was the well staged lecture of Lt. John Quinn of the air force.

Lt. Quinn was one of the thirty-six captured aviators who were hounded into confessing to dropping germ bombs. His confession was not used primarily for propaganda in the outside world as were most.

Instead, after he had been so thoroughly schooled that he himself had begun to believe the fabricated story, he was sent around the circuit of the prisoner of war camps to repeat the tale to G.I. "study groups," and, via loudspeaker, even to those who refused to attend the classes.

"He looked perfectly healthy," a prisoner of war who turned progressive said of that incident. "And there weren't any Chinese around to make him say anything he didn't want to say."

"We just went on about our business and didn't half listen to it," said a reactionary. "We knew what he must have been through to tell a story like that."

Even returned progressives who shamefacedly admit that they were fools to fall for the Red line and now say that "what sounded all right over there doesn't sound so good back home," make an exception of the germ bomb story. They still believe it.

Up to forty days or so before the armistice was signed the whole Communist strategy had been toward two goals: to use prisoners, through their signatures on peace petitions, their letters home and various other devices, to undermine the will to fight of other Americans in Korea; and to indoctrinate as many as they could with Communist ideas to take back with them when they got home.

—22

Up to early June (the armistice was signed on July 26) there had been no suggestion that any American prisoners of war would refuse repatriation. From the beginning of the long armistice negotiations the Communists had fought the whole idea of prisoners being given any choice in the matter. They had demanded forcible repatriation of the North Korean and Chinese prisoners, being held in United Nations prison camps, who had asked asylum.

Eventually they decided they would have to accept non-repatriation if they wanted an armistice, and they wanted an armistice. Evidently around the end of May they decided they had to have some propaganda counter for the fact that thousands of their men would refuse to come back. The time was short to do a full scale job. They decided on a token group, large enough to have some effect on world opinion and small enough to be kept under rigid discipline.

Word sifted through the five prison camps that the Chinese Communists were looking for men who would be willing to stay on their side. Some volunteered—and were refused—and some were selected as candidates who had never even lined up with the "progressives."

They chose them from three groups. First, men with leadership qualities, these to be chosen from among prisoners who had already had some indoctrination. Second, followers for the leaders to direct—the sheep—and these did not need to be good "progressives" under the methods they used, though the majority were. Third, men with deep emotional disturbances, who had broken under prison life.

Those who were chosen were told to write their life stories over and over again until they had written maybe fifty pages. And because they did not know why they were writing, they revealed themselves. It has been said that everyone has something in his life that can be used against him.

Were the twenty-one who stayed particularly vulnerable? Is that why it was that these particular twenty-one, out of the four thousand, will never see home and country? The clues are in the stories of their lives.

Sgt. Richard G. Corden

of Providence, R. I.

born January 2, 1928

re-enlisted March 19, 1950

2nd Division

captured November 30, 1950

Catholic

2 years high school

I.Q. high—134

The Army Reported:

According to returned prisoners of war, Corden volunteered for special duty with the Chinese Communists. As a result, he lived and worked at Chinese headquarters at two different prison camps. He volunteered for and served on a club committee which directed operations at one of the camps. He wrote pro-Communist articles for publication and informed *on his fellow prisoners. His rewards included better living conditions, better food and better medical treatment than that given his fellow prisoners. He is a key figure among the non-repatriates.*

T HE AMERICAN SERGEANT strode up and down the compound like a young Napoleon, throwing back his cape with studied carelessness. Those who got close enough to see his features were appalled by the pervading bitterness of his lean, dark, handsome face.

This was Richard G. Corden, late of Providence, R. I., now leader of the twenty-one American prisoners of war who refused to return to their own country, choosing instead to stay with their Red captors. In the neutral compound at Panmunjom, where, under the armistice terms prisoners who refused repatriation were being held, Corden ruled his men with the arrogance of a corps commander and the relentlessness of a chain gang boss.

He himself was under the constant scrutiny of leaders of the 325 recalcitrant South Koreans who shared the compound.

From September 23 to December 23, during the 3-month period given opposing sides to persuade their countrymen of the folly of their decision, Corden had refused to allow the Americans to leave the compound or listen to explanations. One man of the original twenty-three had managed to slip away. No more chances were being taken.

One of the Indian guards, set up by the armistice to protect the compound, approached the barricades.

"We understand that one of the Americans wants to come out," he said.

Corden flung back his head. "No one comes out," he replied and strode away.

One more did though, in the final month of grace allowed after December 23, but that was all.

When correspondents were permitted into the compound, on January 26, just before the twenty-one left for China, it was Corden who read the long prepared statement:

"We will go back to our homes when the American people are free to enjoy the constitution of 1776 (an error) instead of the Eisenhower-McCarthy constitution of 1954 . . ." it started and went on and on.

Under questioning Corden said, "We are not Communists, but some of us hope to be," and indicated clearly that he at least was one who hoped to be.

Back home, those who loved him wept: his sister who had not seen him since she was twelve, his aunt, his step-grandfather, the mother of a friend with whom he had lived for awhile. There was no one closer than these.

"He was a good boy," said his sister.

"I always loved him. I still love him," said his aunt.

"I don't care what anyone says, he isn't a Communist," said his step-grandfather.

To those who knew him when he entered the service, he was a quiet, handsome boy, brilliant despite lack of formal education, friendly and cooperative, if proud and reserved, who seemed to have recovered from his childhood lacks and teenage difficulties.

But his priest suspected and his aunt knew that the hurts of his childhood were still smoldering beneath that cool exterior; that there was something "unfathomable about him—something you couldn't reach."

—28

Richard Corden was born in Pawtucket, R. I., a suburb of Providence, on September 27, 1928. His father, Lincoln Joseph Corden, was a railroad worker; his nineteen-year-old mother had been born Anna Grace Dunn.

His father's precarious health colored Richard's earliest years. His mother brought him back to the family home when her husband's illness demanded hospitalization and he joined them only in the intervals between hospital stays. There his aunt Kathleen helped her sister care for the boy and learned to love him as her own.

"He was a darling," says his aunt, now Mrs. Henry Mathieu. "But his father's illness had made the man irritable. When he was home he seemed to resent the boy. When Richard was naughty, his father would beat him unmercifully with the buckle end of a belt. Dick learned to stand and take it without a tear, even though he knew the beating would go on until he did cry. It was only when his mother broke down and went to pieces that he would weaken and cry. He was only a little more than three when he ran away after one of those beatings."

Corden's sister, Ursula Jean, was born when he was five and a half and Mrs. Corden never quite recovered her strength afterward. She died of pneumonia in February, 1935; three months later her husband died in a hospital in Portland, Me.

His mother's death left a deep impression on the six-year-old boy. Richard could not forget the picture of her in her coffin. To his aunt, months later, he spoke of how beautiful she looked, how pretty her hair was; and he described every detail of the dress she was laid out in.

His father had left a small estate in trust for the children. His will named Richard's paternal grandmother as guardian.

Ursula had already been taken by her grandmother during Mrs. Corden's illness but the boy didn't want to leave his aunt.

For nearly a year he was allowed to stay in Pawtucket but the day finally came when he had to go to the apartment in East Providence where his sister and step-grandfather still live.

It is second floor rear of an old frame building in an area zoned for business. There is a showroom for milking equipment on the first floor. The buildings face a traffic turnaround and the approach to the bridge that leads from East Providence to Providence proper.

There are few neighbors, none that were here when Richard came to live. His grandmother (she died while he was overseas) had remarried and her husband, Patrick J. O'Connor, a day laborer, evidently accepted Richard as he might have accepted a grandson of his own.

His obvious fondness for Richard was tinged with bitterness when I came to see him, now it was certain that the boy had made his final choice to stay with the Communists.

"We're through," he said with a harshness that was foreign to him. "We're through with him. He's dead as far as we're concerned. It would have been better if he had been shot. He could have come home. He had his chance to come home and he didn't take it."

And then memories came crowding to the small, slight, pallid old man and he forgot the present.

"He was a quiet one, all right. There never was any harm in him. He was a bright one too. Maybe he didn't get to college but he had as good an education as those boys up on the Hill (Brown University). Why, when they had a spelling bee down here at the theater—they had it on the radio—we

—30

listened and he could outspell all of them. He read a lot of books, big books, books for grownups."

Earlier, while there was still hope that he would come back, O'Connor talked more freely of Richard's childhood—of how he used to stand at the window and look down at the brick-covered street and watch the other boys playing. Sometimes, he would go down, sometimes just watch.

"He'd play with them all right. But they would have to ask him. He was not a boy to push his way into things. He was a boy who always did what he was told without grumbling. I remember I used to send him all the way to Six Corners to get something at the store and he would never give me one of those frowns like so many kids do."

Despite these memories, it is clear that Richard was not happy at the East Providence apartment. His grandmother did not share her husband's pride in Richard's interest in books. She thought he read too much and wouldn't let him have a light in his room at night.

That was unimportant compared to his loneliness for his aunt who was his last link to his mother and his loneliness for her home which he thought of as his real home. When that loneliness became unbearable he would slip out and find his way back to Pawtucket.

"His grandparents didn't have a phone then," his aunt recalled, "and we couldn't get word to them right away that Richard was with us. And he would miss school. So the truant officer and the child welfare authorities came in on it.

"I wanted to keep Richard. And maybe they would have let me," Mrs. Mathieu said, "but my husband had died recently and my father was old and we were having a hard time financially. So they put him in a foster home and that's when the trouble started."

Father James Lamb, now of St. Mary's parish in Pawtucket, but in those days with Sacred Heart parish in East Providence, remembers that period.

"There was something about the boy you couldn't touch," he said. "I was trying to help keep him out of the state training school. He had stolen some trinkets—ornaments off of cars. He seemed normal and healthy, but he had a way of withdrawing. He was a lively boy—and then he would go into his shell. You talked to him—but you did not always feel that you could reach him. There was something unfathomable about him, some deep hurt that you couldn't get to."

Despite Father Lamb's interest, the day came when Richard was sent to the state training school. Rhode Island laws make it mandatory that no information as to reason for entrance, length of stay or record at the school be given out. But it is known that Richard's infractions of the law were never more serious than the charge of stealing trinkets off cars.

"He just got in with the wrong gang of little fellows," his step-grandfather commented. "There never was any harm in him."

Richard ran away from the training school when he was fifteen and got himself a job as a welder at the Kaiser-Walsh shipyards which were going full tilt in 1943. He found himself a room at the YMCA. Juvenile authorities traced him there but let him alone. With his first week's pay he bought a record player and started collecting the classical records that were his hobby and his solace.

His school days were over. They hadn't amounted to much. He had gone to four different schools up to the eighth grade, two public schools in Pawtucket: Sacred Heart Parochial and East Providence Junior High in East Providence.

What grades he made were better than average and his I.Q. test, taken at the training school, gave him the unusually high score of 134, highest of all the twenty-one.

Richard made a friend while he worked at the shipyards, Edward Fontaine, and for a time he knew what it was to live in the midst of a warm and close-knit family circle even if it wasn't his own. He got the flu the first winter he worked and Edward brought him home to his mother, Mrs. Eugenie Fontaine. She nursed him back to health and he stayed on afterward, playing the records he loved with Edward's kid sister Jeanette and taking part in the evening gatherings of young people drawn to this hospitable hearth.

Richard began to call Mrs. Fontaine "Mom" and later when he was in prison camp wrote to her as "Mom." But of his own mother and her death, he could not bring himself to speak.

"He was a quiet boy," Mrs. Fontaine told me. "But I didn't think he was a sad boy. He never gave us any trouble. He loved music and he was a great reader. Nobody in his right mind would ever believe that Richard would turn Communist."

With the end of the war, the work at the shipyards fell off abruptly and soon the plant was closed down entirely. Richard tried to get into the navy, was turned down because of his eyesight, and enlisted for a four-year hitch in the army in March of 1946.

"He enlisted because he wanted to get off the local scene," Father Lamb, who was still in touch with him, told me.

"He wanted to go places and see things; he wanted adventure," said his cousin.

Because of his high intelligence rating, Richard was eligible for officers' training. Investigators for the army came to Providence and talked to his relatives and friends about his juvenile record. Evidently the stay at the state training school stood against him. He didn't get the chance to go to OCS.

After basic training he came back on leave and went to stay with his aunt in Pawtucket. He got along well with his cousin Arlene who was close to him in age. They had good times together.

"Girls were always attracted to him," Arlene said. "He was quiet and good-looking and a neat dresser and he danced well. But he didn't date a lot and he didn't have any special girl that I knew of."

He paid a visit to his grandparents' home and saw his sister, then twelve years old, for the last time. He asked for foreign service and was sent to Germany in the Occupation Army. But before that he had gone AWOL and been convicted and fined $50. And he had met a girl. Here the record is blurred. Perhaps they were engaged. Anyway, he got a "Dear John" letter while he was in Germany, breaking off the romance. His barracks mates said that he changed after that and became even more silent and morose.

He started dating girls in Berlin and then one in particular, who was attached to the American embassy there. His enlistment was almost up and he made plans to leave the army and get a job so he could earn enough money to post a bond for the girl and her mother.

Back home in the spring of 1950, on his last leave before his enlistment was up, he stayed with the Fontaines. Friends who saw him then remarked on his restlessness. He tried to see his aunt but she had moved and he couldn't find her. He didn't go to his old home in East Providence or see his sister. He bought a car and had a minor accident when the hood flew up while he was driving.

During his overseas service Richard had taken correspondence courses and gotten his high school credits. He had talked of going on to college and becoming a chemist. Suddenly he talked of making a career of the army. No one knows what happened about the girl in Berlin. He had confided little about her to begin with. All they know is that on March 17, 1950, the day his enlistment was up, he re-enlisted and asked for Tokyo duty.

He got it. He was in Seattle the day the Korean fighting started and he went over with the 2nd Division to get into the fighting early that summer. On November 30 he was captured, along with nearly half of his fellow non-repatriates, when the Chinese hordes came down in full force.

Returned prisoners of war have said that Corden was an early convert of the Reds who quickly became a "big wheel" at Communist headquarters. Here he found the recognition of his abilities he had never found, either in civilian life or in the army. The pride that had kept him from crying when his father beat him as a child, that had held him aloof from the neighborhood children in East Providence, and made him unreachable as he got into his teens, now had something to feed on.

Most prisoners of war said he kept to himself, even in camp, and did not bother to argue others into becoming progressives. One said that the Chinese had gotten to him by giving him marijuana to smoke; another that Corden had told him he had believed in Communism before his capture.

If that was true it was certainly not in his Providence days. His disinterest in politics of any sort had been complete, all those who knew him there insisted. And the letters they received from him in prison camp did not follow the propaganda line as did those received by families and friends of many prisoners of war, including some who did not stay with their captors.

It was true that he asked his sister and his cousin to pray for peace and once wrote that the American people ought to get together and fight for peace, but these pleas were coupled with a description of the hardships of prison camp life, of how he "dreaded going through another winter with insufficient clothing." Later he wrote that the food and clothing were a little better.

His last letter to his aunt sounded "blue." He wondered if he would ever get out of prison and said if he did get back he wanted to marry and settle down to a career in the army at a post near Providence.

His last letter to Mrs. Fontaine was more specific.

"Dear Mom," he wrote, "I hope this letter finds all of you in good health. Will you have a wife ready for me when I get home? I definitely intend to settle down when I get back and I can't think of a better way to do it than through the institution of marriage. Take good care of yourself, Mom, for life is short—too short to waste. God bless you all."

Shortly after that letter was written he was approached to be one of the group to refuse repatriation. He never wrote another letter home.

A local broadcasting station got together some of Richard's friends and relatives to make a recording to be sent in to him during the period of grace when he might change his mind.

Father Lamb, Mrs. Fontaine, Ursula Jean and Patrick O'Connor were among them.

"Dick, this is Jean," said his sister. "It is now that I need you most because I am all alone and you are the only one I can turn to."

Corden refused to hear the recording—as did the others whose families made similar attempts to reach them.

"I have thought so much about what prompted Richard

to do this," Father Lamb told me. "He was a boy who never had anything, who didn't have much to be happy about. He was a wonderfully bright boy and he showed definite signs of qualities of leadership. But he had little direction. True, he read a great deal, but only what he wanted to read. He had no knowledge of Communism or the nature of propaganda. I haven't got the answer but I feel that it is a further development of something he suffered when he was a child. I think that if we had had the staff then, and psychiatric advice, he could have been helped. He must be confused now. No boy in his right senses would do what he did."

Richard took his troupe with him behind the Iron Curtain in January, 1954. There has been an occasional picture, a vagrant voice on a monitored radio broadcast from one or another of the twenty-one. But from Richard Corden no word at all.

Pfc. William A. Cowart

    of Dalton, Ga.

born January 10, 1933

    enlisted January 7, 1949

24th Division

    captured July 12, 1950

Protestant

    3 years high school

average I.Q.

The Army Reported:

According to returned prisoners of war, he ingratiated himself with the Chinese Communists by volunteering to write articles for the Communist publication Toward Truth and Peace *and by making propaganda recordings. While he had no special or regular duties, he aided the Chinese by writing for Communist publications, by* informing on fellow prisoners, and by preaching Communism among them. He was convinced by the Chinese that collaborating with them would insure a fruitful and happy life.

"**I** HAVE LEARNED a very valuable lesson since becoming a prisoner of war and that is that education is a very wonderful thing. I only wish that I had continued mine when I had a chance."

These sentiments were expressed by William Cowart of Dalton, Ga., in a letter he wrote from prison camp to the students and faculty of the high school he quit to enlist in the army. If Billy Cowart had reason to regret his precipitate exit from student life then, he has even more cause now that he is a man without a country, doomed to live out his life a stranger in a strange land.

"I've gone too far; I can't go back," he told the only man in his hut still on speaking terms with him since he had become a progressive. That was just before the armistice was signed ending the Korean war.

"He came over and told me that he had just been to regimental headquarters and had agreed to refuse repatriation," James Wilson of Chattanooga, Tenn., a returned prisoner of war, said. "I tried to argue him out of it. But he said it was too late; that he didn't have any friends anyway; that no one would talk to him. I never saw him again."

What happened to bring this sturdy, handsome Georgia boy, who gave his mother no peace until she signed his enlistment papers, to the point of no return?

Wilson only knew the surface details.

"I met him in the winter of 1950," he told me. "He had been a prisoner since the beginning of the war and had been in a hospital because of malnutrition. We got caught stealing food one night from the warehouse and we got beaten, like they always did to the prisoners of war who stole food. But he only got beaten the once. After that they would just talk to him when they caught him and he went back night after night.

"The boys knew someone was informing on them. Cowart was in the good treatment class and it looked like he was the one. No one would speak to him any more. We had a big fight in the compound once—the progressives, pro-Chinese against the rest of us. After that he took to going up to regimental headquarters and staying there most of the time!"

Dalton, Ga., where Bill Cowart was born and grew up, looks at first glance like any sleepy southern town, with its broad main street, its antebellum hotel, and its stores advertising turnip seed and rye grass.

Nestled in the hills on Highway 41, closer to Chattanooga than to Atlanta, it is in fact anything but sleepy. A bustling mill town, heart of the long-booming chenille bedspread industry, Dalton is, in fact, the place where the old candlewick spread had its rebirth. On all the roads leading into town bright-colored samples flap in the breeze on long lines strung out by farm "outlet" stores set out between fancy motels advertising air conditioning and television sets.

The business in bedspreads and chenille throw rugs amounts to $200,000,000 a year but except for the thread and yarn factories which supply it, the signs of industry are hard to find. Most of the chenille plants are set up in sheds and barns, back from the side roads. Cheap current from TVA powers the sewing machines and the women of the town, largely, run them.

William A. Cowart

Mothers of half of the children enrolled in the schools work on the spreads. School overcrowding problems are met by putting fifty to sixty in a classroom rather than by shifts, since the schools find themselves in the position of having to watch over the children while their mothers work.

"The mushroom growth of Dalton in the past twenty-five years has more than tripled the population," one teacher said. "Those who got in on the ground floor of the chenille industry have become extremely wealthy. The others work for that industry. It's a situation of those who have and those who have not—and the teachers are in the middle."

Billy's parents worked in the mills and when Billy was old enough he worked there after school himself. An only child and adored by his mother, Bill's childhood was clouded by the trouble which led to a break between his father and mother, culminating in a divorce when he was six. He saw his father only once more, when he was fourteen.

"He ducked his head down, like he often did when there were adults around," a neighbor recalled, "and ran out of the house and didn't come back until his father had left."

Not long after that he ran away from home. He was discovered in Ohio, the state where his father had gone to live, though neither Billy nor anyone else knew exactly where.

After the divorce, Mrs. Cowart married her present husband, Chester Green, who tried to be a father to his young stepson and according to friends did "everything he could for the boy and treated him as though he were his own."

At school, however, the effects of Billy's reaction to having a stepfather were apparent.

"He had quite a few emotional problems to solve," one teacher said. "It was apparent that he had a chip on his shoulder and, from things he said in class, that he didn't get along with his stepfather. He was extremely insecure and rather than make friends and fail, he just withdrew from the other boys in the class."

Billy's I.Q. was rated average, but he was in the lower quarter of his class and had failed three subjects when he left school. If he had stayed he would not have been able to graduate with his class.

"He did not seem to dislike school," C. E. Bowen, principal of Dalton High School, said. "But he must have toward the end because he made such efforts to get out. He was a boy who was hard to know. At times he was easy to talk to and would cooperate. At other times he was silent and resentful—suspicious."

This dualism was noticed by most of his teachers, who called him moody—now stubborn, now docile; sometimes responsive, at others apathetic. One day he would work hard, the next day sit and stare. If he wanted to be polite and cooperative, no one could be more so but he didn't always want to be. If he made a bad grade, it was the teacher's fault; it was a "rotten" school. If he was feeling in the mood he would pat the teacher on the back and tell her she was the best in the school.

"He pretended he didn't care about people but he really wanted to be popular," one teacher said. "He just went about it in the wrong way. In his attempt to stand out he only made himself look foolish. He would wear odd clothes, hats with trinkets or bells on them to get attention. Or he would stay outside the classroom until after the bell rang so he could get noticed by being late."

One teacher was not much surprised at the news that Billy was one of the twenty-one. "I felt that if anyone I had ever taught would do that, he would be the one," she said. "It may be that he did it to get the attention he wanted—and he couldn't see how shallow and short-lived it was."

Another teacher spoke of "how much it would have gratified us when he was in school to have known that he could even identify national figures," when she was told of his statement, typical of the twenty-one, about "McCarthyism and McCarranism."

I went to talk to Miss Mattie Lee Huff, dean of Dalton's teachers, in the beautiful old home, once headquarters for General Johnston during the Civil War, where she and her sisters live. Billy had brought her a present—a china dog—which she still treasures, before he left for training camp.

Miss Huff taught in the Dalton schools for fifty years, from third grade on through high school. Though she never had Billy in her classes, he used to drop into her room after school and talk to her; she is that kind of person.

Tiny and gracious with a warmth she does not ration out merely to the "deserving," she shook her head sadly as she talked of Billy.

"It breaks my heart," she said, "to think how utterly we have failed in that boy."

Although Billy was big for his age and unusually good-looking he never took any part in school activities or athletics; he didn't belong to any clubs, he wasn't in the school play, he tried out for no teams.

One of the girls with whom he went to school pointed out rather bitterly that kids from the mills didn't have a chance against kids from the Hill when it came to getting any place in the school's social life.

Billy had no pals in school; he wouldn't let any of the other boys get close to him. But he had a girl and they went steady—at least at school. Going steady at Dalton means meeting after every class and escorting your girl to the next, eating lunch with her, carrying her books home. Billy didn't date her much evenings, though he went to church with her and talked to her for hours after school on a neighbor's phone, when he wasn't working.

Billy Cowart enlisted in the army in January of 1949, a few days before he was sixteen, according to his mother; seventeen, according to the army. He was in the 24th Infantry Division and was one of the first American soldiers to be put in the front lines and one of the first to be taken prisoner— less than three weeks after the start of the Korean hostilities.

Because of his early capture Cowart had a longer period of semi-starvation than those who were captured later when rations became somewhere near subsistence level. On the other hand he was one of the earliest progressives in his camp and as such was an outcast to the prisoners who did not collaborate with the Chinese. His loneliness was attested by the fantastic number of letters he wrote from prison camp. He kept up a correspondence with a group of teenagers who had been but ten or twelve when he left home, little sisters of the girls that had been his classmates. He wrote to everyone he knew sooner or later.

He even wrote a nostalgic letter to his former employer, J. F. Calloway, Jr.

"I'll never forget you people," Billy wrote on the stationery supplied by the Chinese People's Committee for World Peace, stamped with the Picasso Dove. "All you folks drop me a line once in a while. I know you are busy most of the time but just a short note and maybe a photograph or two helps 100 per cent here."

The letter looks as though it had been written by two different people but there is a simple explanation for that. The first few lines are written in a fancy slanted script with circles for dots and flourishes on the y's. Then it breaks down into a scribble but there are still occasional circles and flourishes.

It might be that the effort to write a stylish hand became too tiresome.

Calloway wrote Billy a letter after it was known that he was one of the group who had chosen to stay with the Chinese Communists. It was full of reminders of pleasant times, hunting and fishing trips, movies they had seen, an invitation to "a big shindig when you get home" and a promise that a job would be waiting for him.

Calloway, who was in the Signal Corps in World War II, is fond of Billy and feels that anyone who hasn't been subjected to imprisonment and torture is not in a position to condemn those who cracked under it.

"Bill was just a kid and he was wounded," Calloway said. "Remember that. Even those who came back didn't know what they were fighting for. As for Billy, he hardly knew who was President. Perhaps the loss of his father had an effect on him. If under the stress and strain those twenty-one broke, even if they caused other prisoners to be persecuted because they broke, you must consider the conditions they were under."

Calloway is working with Dalton's Chamber of Commerce on an Americanization program and a recreation plan for the boys now growing up in Dalton; he feels there is a real need for both. It is too late for Billy Cowart, of course.

Billy wrote his first letter to one of the home town girls after his mother wrote him that his "steady" had gotten married while he was in camp. How much of a shock that was to him is hard to assess.

His cabin mate, Wilson, recalled that about the time he received it he swam far out into the lake near camp with the idea of committing suicide, but changed his mind and came back.

Still he was quite casual in his mention of his former girl

when he wrote to Rhoda Ann Hayes, who was ten when he enlisted.

"I guess I am out in the cold since Estelle got married," he wrote, "but I have still got Mom to love." In a later letter he spoke of the "spree" he would go on when he got home, adding:

"I would very much like to have a nursemaid to hold my aching head afterward. There's only one requirement. Don't be married."

In a letter to another girl, written February 15, 1953, he said, "I go along completely with your hopes for our release and repatriation. I think all the boys do."

Most of his letters spoke of his homesickness; occasionally he spoke of the "peace movement" and the good treatment and "cooperation of the Chinese." Here is a typical one:

Hi Cutie:

I am sitting here on my buddy's bunk drinking hot tea and listening to a couple of the boys out in the kitchen playing and singing. It's a hot day, the sun is blazing now. A quite warm day, sure starts a guy to thinking and when this happens to me I always get a severe case of homesickness.

Just think of all the wonderful things I could be doing today at home. Dancing, swimming, driving. A beautiful little gal like you for a companion, a few bottles of cold beer, soft music. I wonder if I'll ever live again.

All that taken because of the Korea conflict. Nearly three years now and nearly two of that in truce talks. The only problem left is one point on the prisoner of war issue. I wonder if they are going to wait until all we boys go crazy or die of old age before they finally end this thing.

This latest proposal by Chou En-lai of the Chinese side looks like it should be the answer to both sides' problems. I guess the talks started back today. I hope something comes of it.

Something did, but not quite what Billy had been counting on then. That was his last letter home. Billy was tapped to be one of the twenty-one—"I've gone too far; I can't go back."

Billy's mother, who cried herself to sleep for long months after she heard the news and whose health broke down under the strain of worrying over her son, takes consolation only in the thought that this boy is not really her boy, not really the Billy Cowart who marched off from Dalton so proudly in 1949.

I talked to her in Monticello, Ark., where her husband had taken her to get away and recover her health, finding himself a job there. She is a pretty, gentle-faced woman, who is taking care of her nephew now, a boy not much older than Billy was when he left but who doesn't seem to have Billy's problems.

"I'm sure that boy in the pictures isn't Bill," she says. "That boy has a lock of hair falling over his forehead and my Bill had a cowlick and he wasn't that heavy."

If that was her boy, Mrs. Green felt that maybe the news that his girl had gotten married might have affected him.

"And then if they told him he would be arrested when he came back to this country, he would have stayed over there because Billy had a horror of being arrested," Mrs. Green said. "He was afraid of the police. But I don't think it was him."

Looking back on Billy's life, Mrs. Green feels that she left him alone too much and depended on him too much: "He did most of the housework after school because my husband and I were at the mills. And then he worked too, at the mill and at a sandwich shop because he wanted to earn his own money."

Opinion in his home town is divided.

"He was not a boy I would have picked out as being one who would turn his allegiance from his country," Principal Bowen said.

"I wasn't a bit surprised," said a neighbor. "Billy was a strange boy, never happy or satisfied in his life. I can't say that I ever liked him, though he was in and out of my house most of his life. But when I saw the movies of him over there, I sat down and cried."

"He was a nice kid with great pride in his appearance," said another. "He was quiet and moody; he tried to be happy-go-lucky but he just couldn't make it. I think he was just too young. They shouldn't have sent him over there that young."

Billy danced a jig for South Korean prisoners of war just before he left for the interior of China. Since then there has been silence. If he has danced any more jigs they aren't being photographed.

Pfc. Lowell Denver Skinner

                    of Akron, O.

born April 9, 1931

               enlisted 1949

1st Cavalry

        captured November 2, 1950

Protestant

       8th grade

average I.Q.

The Army Reported:

According to returned prisoners of war, Skinner assisted Communist political instructors, disseminated propaganda material among prisoners and attempted to convert them to Communism, wrote articles for the publication Toward Truth and Peace, *made propaganda recordings and became an* informer. *His rewards included better treatment, better food and clothing and better medical attention.*

Lowell D. Skinner

"**I** AM GOING TO CHINA to fight for peace," said the poker-faced American in the padded blue Chinese uniform.

"How, exactly, do you fight for peace?" asked the correspondent.

"You speak out for it."

"What do you say?"

"You oppose war, you support peace."

"How do you support peace?"

"You speak out for it."

There was little point in going round and round that barn again so the interview was terminated. Shortly afterward, Lowell Skinner, the boy who ate bananas for a week so he he could get up to 116 pounds and be accepted by the army, set out for China with the rest of the twenty-one prisoners of war who refused to come home.

Lowell Denver Skinner was remembered by his neighbors in the river bottoms west of Akron, O., where he grew up, and by his teachers as "the boy who never smiled." His mother, who refused to sign for an underage enlistment and prayed that he wouldn't pass the physical when he enlisted on his own at eighteen, agreed that Lowell couldn't do better than "a sort of half smile" even when he tried.

His last letter home, written in January of 1954 but not delivered for six months, told of a series of illnesses he had undergone.

"Mom," he wrote, "I've been pretty sick. My teeth went bad and an infection set in my jaw. The entire right side of my head and jaw swelled up and they gave me penicillin. It was after that I had pneumonia twice and malaria. But I'm all right now except my teeth. I haven't any jaw teeth and it presents a problem while eating."

Looking at his picture in the groups taken at Panmunjom, Mrs. Brady Skinner wasn't sure it was her boy. His hair was too dark and his nose too large. There was a "resemblance," she allowed; this boy certainly wasn't smiling so you couldn't see whether he had all his teeth or not.

"But his face doesn't look like he had lost all those teeth and I can't see the Communists giving him false teeth," she told me.

"How do we know that those men are our boys?" Mrs. Skinner added. "You know that mother that flew to Japan and then wasn't allowed to see her son? I think the Communists were afraid to let her. She would have found out that those men aren't our boys at all."

Still, the Skinners were convinced enough to make a recording, as nearly all families did in the vain hope that their boy would hear it and it would influence him to come home.

"Please Lowell, listen to me," Mrs. Skinner pleaded. "You must come home. You are needed here, son. I have waited for you for almost three years and I have always stood by you. Please son, don't let me down. I can't give you up. I love you."

To this his father added, "I need you too, Lowell. Make it as quick as possible."

The Skinner family knew very early that their son had become a progressive.

His letters went further than most. In addition to criticizing the Korean conflict as "a senseless waste of lives and

property" he asked his parents to withdraw $50 he had in a savings bank and send it to the *New Masses* and the *Daily Worker*.

"Not only do these magazines serve the working classes by printing the truth," he wrote, "but they help unite the people in their peace fight. I also hope you write the *Worker* and voice your appreciation."

The Skinners didn't carry out Lowell's request, of course. His letters didn't sound like he had written them himself but like someone had "dictated" them, they thought. "They were full of big words he never used." And then, too, there was the letter he had written before he ever was captured.

"Mom," he wrote then, "if anything ever happens and I should be captured, don't believe anything they tell you. Don't sign any papers—you can't trust some people, you know."

That bulwarks them in their intermittent hope that this may all turn out to be a hoax and Lowell will come walking down the road one day.

Lowell, the first boy in his family—he has two older sisters, one younger sister and a younger brother—was "the apple of my eye," his mother told me. When he was little the family lived on a farm in central Ohio but moved to Akron about the time he started school.

His father, a World War I veteran—a cavalryman—works as a plasterer. The family live in an unprepossessing tarpaper shack, not much larger than an oversize trailer, set in a field far back from the road on the outskirts of Akron. The Skinners resent newspaper and magazine references to their home as substandard.

Neighbors also are unhappy over the description, and point out that if a family has had to spend money on "medical bills instead of home beautification" that should not be held against them.

These same neighbors thought Lowell "a good little kid, bullheaded maybe—he had a mind of his own and he wanted to do it his way or he wouldn't do it."

"His parents did everything they could for their kids," another neighbor said. "When Lowell got in trouble for shooting that deer out on his uncle's place in Wyoming one summer, his mother made the trip all the way out there to stand by him."

"That was the only time he was ever in trouble, and that wasn't what you'd call serious trouble," a former employer commented. "Lowell was a good worker, a serious-minded boy."

The family moved about a good deal and Lowell went to four different schools in Akron. He repeated the first grade and although his I.Q. was in the average range, 103, and his achievement tests showed him above average in reading and vocabulary as well as social science, his grades were generally low, though his work habits and conduct were marked "Good."

The only teacher who remembered him called him a "poker face"—the child who never smiled.

"He did his work, but nothing extra; did what was expected of him but that was all," she said. "He was never chosen by the other children to do anything—and he didn't care if they didn't."

He was fifteen when he started first year high school and he only attended fifty-four days, not time enough for any teacher to get acquainted with him or the high school's guidance program to come into effect. Again it was noted that among the pictures taken of the class, his was the only unsmiling face.

Lowell D. Skinner

His mother said he left school because "it was too hard for him," though he loved to read if it was about anything mechanical. He learned to repair watches and to make model guns; he worked for the local store, cared for the greens of the local golf course and did odd jobs.

Even before he left school he had earned his pocket money. If he wanted fifty cents he wouldn't ask for it, he'd find a way to earn it. He worked and bought bikes for both himself and his younger brother, selling papers, running errands.

I talked to the Skinners in the kitchen of their compact home, sitting around the kitchen table. Mrs. Skinner is a naturally cheerful person, hurt and bewildered now by all that has gone on since the announcement about her son. Her husband is mild mannered; quiet, but with strong opinions.

Lowell was always small for his age, they said, and while he played with the boys in the neighborhood, had no special pal and didn't care for organized sports. He loved to ride his bike and would go off on thirty- or forty-mile jaunts by himself. He always got home on time when he said he would. He was the same way about getting back to camp when he was on leave and went to extreme lengths to make sure he would get back on time and have a clean record.

He didn't lose his temper easily, and would usually walk out before an argument really got started. He was slow to get into physical combat but when he did "he went all out" his father said, proudly, recalling a time when the sheriff came round with two big boys who said Lowell had beaten up both of them.

His parents felt that they had always tried to be fair with him—he got his share of whippings, mostly for taking his older sisters' things, but nothing was saved up to be told on him at the end of the day. "I never did believe in cold punishment," his father said.

When he was fourteen Lowell fell down the stairs and fractured his back and he had a serious case of yellow jaundice when he was a little younger, but no other serious illnesses until prison camp.

The Skinners have some theories as to what happened to Lowell in Korea.

"I don't know what Communism is, frankly," Skinner said, "but I know I don't want to live under a dictatorship. Sometimes at work the men get to talking about it and if they argue for having a stronger government my answer is: No government ever created a man, but men create governments and have the right to change them. No country, no family, no person can exclude himself from the world.

"If Lowell had been interested just once in politics he would have learned all about it and this wouldn't have happened to him. But he was young and he wasn't interested and they don't teach it in school."

The court-martials of Dickenson and Batchelor, Skinner felt, were unfair and would make it likely that in the future other boys would choose to stay over rather than come back.

"They were loyal soldiers up to the time of their capture. If under the torture of starvation and lack of medical attention these boys broke, it should be taken into consideration."

Frank Noel, the AP photographer who was captured and imprisoned along with the troops, visited the Skinner family to try to bring them some solace. He had known Lowell in camp and told his parents that even to get an aspirin a prisoner of war had to sign a peace petition—and Lowell had been mighty sick.

Mrs. Skinner finds it hard to accept that "you are responsible for what your boy does if you let him drive a car at nineteen but the army can take him and send him out to kill and be killed without your say-so."

Lowell D. Skinner

Lowell was eighteen when he enlisted on August 16, 1949, without his parents' signatures. The banana diet worked and he passed his physical. He was in Japan when the hostilities started in Korea. He had wanted to be in the cavalry like his father, and had been transferred to the 8th Regiment, 1st Cavalry Division just before going overseas. Only now it was an infantry division retaining only the proud old title.

The 1st Cavalry Division landed at Pohang in South Korea on July 18 and was immediately rushed by truck into battle against the North Koreans. It helped turn the tide and was one of the divisions that rushed on to the North Korean capital of Pyongyang late in October. Victory seemed assured and the 1st Cavalry began making plans for a victory march in Tokyo on Armistice Day. Then, on Hallowe'en, under a full moon, Chinese Communists with Russian burp guns attacked in force for the first time. The 8th Regiment was surrounded and eight hundred men cut off for two days. Many were dead or wounded. Some were allowed to escape without a shot being fired at them. Lowell Skinner was captured— officially reported missing on November 2, 1950.

Fellow prisoners reported that he "played ball with the Reds" early in his imprisonment but were surprised when he decided to stay. One thought he really wanted to come home "but is afraid of something."

When a correspondent asked him that last day if he had any message to send to his folks, Lowell replied stiffly: "No message. In a little while I will write and explain to them. I'm sure they have faith in me." Then he faltered a moment and added, "Tell them I am in good health. Tell them not to worry."

Cpl. LaRance Sullivan

                    Santa Barbara, Calif.

born February 1, 1931

                    enlisted February 25, 1948

2nd Division

                    captured November 25, 1950

Negro, Protestant

                    3rd year high school

average I.Q.

The Army Reported:

According to returned prisoners of war, Sullivan was a member of the staff of the camp news-paper for which he wrote articles extolling Communism. He circulated petitions and urged his fellow prisoners to sign them, made propaganda recordings for broadcast, attempted to convert his fellow prisoners to Communism, and was placed in charge of a group of prisoners as one of his rewards.

You cannot find anyone in Santa Barbara who is willing to condemn LaRance Sullivan for turning his back on America or on their fair town, sprawling along the hills that edge the Pacific midway between San Francisco and Los Angeles.

It's not because they don't realize the enormity of the step he has taken.

It's not because they were so fond of him, though those who knew him could not but respond to his infectious grin, his laughter and his clowning antics.

It's because they know too much about his background.

They know about the crowded slum where he lived in such contrast to the general opulence of their town.

They know about the little boy who was so hungry "he ate out of garbage cans" and did not have "the habit of breakfast."

They know about the boy—older now—who shepherded his younger sisters into the haven of a police station when the drinking parties at home became too terrifying.

They know about the succession of stepfathers and the one in particular who beat his mother and persuaded her to sign his enlistment "so we can be rid of him."

And they know how his loyalty to his mother never wavered—and what her end was.

"The first thing my brother wanted to do when he got out of the army was to get Mother started on a new road, get her a home and everything. Even as a little boy he always made plans of how we would do for Mother. . . . And nothing turned out right."

Mrs. Anita Palmore turned to hush her little boy, then stared out of the window of her neat apartment high on a hill in a federal housing project across the Bay from San Francisco.

"Things are worse than ever now," she said without emphasis. "But I guess he had his reasons."

Whatever his reasons, LaRance Vance Sullivan, alone out of the twenty-one who refused repatriation and stayed with their Red captors, expressed one reason he did not learn completely out of a Communist copybook.

"I have heard about my mother," Sullivan told a correspondent just before he went behind the Iron Curtain. "If our living conditions had been better, this need not have happened."

What happened to LaRance's mother—and what happened to him—began thirty odd years ago when a little girl named Laura Mae was abandoned by her mother in Oklahoma.

"My parents left me a little money when they died," Mrs. Mary B. Frost, tiny, wizened and frail, just home from the hospital, told me. "Laura Mae's mother wouldn't do for her, so I adopted her. I put her through high school. I would have sent her to college but then she fell in love and got married. They went to Denver and LaRance was born there. Then Laura Mae's husband left her. I was in California so Laura Mae came to me here."

Mrs. Frost rocked and inhaled camphor in the miniature living room of her miniature apartment in a rear house in Ventura, thirty miles south of Santa Barbara.

"Laura Mae never cared much for staying home," Mrs. Frost said, "so the boy was with me a lot. He was a bright boy, he was a good boy, he was such a nice little guy. That's why it hurt me so much when he said he wasn't coming home."

Mrs. Frost brushed a tear from her furrowed brown cheek. "We were as poor as Job's turkey most of the time but LaRance didn't give me no trouble. Only time I ever had to spank him in his life was when he was six and like to set fire to my house. He was well liked and respected by white folks too."

That was not just a fond grandmother's illusion about her favorite grandson. LaRance was a tall, handsome, outwardly sunny-dispositioned, likable lad, always laughing, always clowning. Still, he worked hard at whatever jobs he could get as a boy and he trained stubbornly at the Santa Barbara Boys' Club to achieve fifty-five chin-ups in succession and thus become National Champion of the Boys' Clubs of America.

All was not well behind that cheerful façade. Teachers and welfare workers, police, probation officers and Boys' Club directors knew it, and did what they could.

"The resources of the community are richer now," says Dr. Charlotte Elmott, director of child guidance, "and in today's Santa Barbara, the case of LaRance Sullivan might have turned out differently."

Even as it was, more attention was paid to LaRance's handicaps than would have been in most American cities. He was first referred to the child guidance clinic when he was seven and in the first grade, because he stuttered and was having difficulty learning.

It was then that his home situation was first discovered. Attempts were made from time to time to better it. Living conditions were poor, welfare workers reported; there was overcrowding and no privacy; Mrs. Sullivan could not handle the discipline problems of the children; they did not get enough to eat.

LaRance was given an intelligence test and found to be of "good average intelligence." Still, he did not do well in school. His personality tests showed he had little confidence in his own judgment or his own abilities, that he was co-operative, but not a leader; was stimulated by approval and resented discipline.

"LaRance has not got the security that makes for good adjustment," child guidance experts reported. "This insecurity has existed over a period of years and has already built up personality traits that will require close supervision. He can be appealed to and he responds but it will have to be done often."

Most of his teachers noted that he was inaccurate and a careless worker; his shop teacher thought he would do better as a "clown rather than a shop man"; but his art teacher said he had "a distinctive, if primitive style, all his own."

His teachers recognized that LaRance's clowning was his way of winning the attention he could get no other way.

"He was never belittled in class," said Mrs. Zelma Pierce, his English teacher and counselor in high school. "The other children loved to have him put on one of his acts of pantomime or mimicry. He liked to have his name pronounced as if it were La Rance, and we did."

Mrs. Pierce added that while LaRance read well and interpreted well what he read, "we always felt that he had greater possibilities than he was showing. Of course he had no time for studying and home conditions interfered with his progress. I was sorry for LaRance in that he didn't have the home and the love he should have had. He had a great need for recognition. I can't imagine anything worse than the childhood he experienced.

—66

"We have other children here with the same racial background, the same economic background and similar physical conditions but they have not had his difficulties in adjusting to the world because despite all else, the home was a warm and secure place."

During World War II, LaRance's mother got a job in an aircraft plant working nights at seventy-five cents an hour. At that time LaRance was found dancing for pennies in front of the USO late at night. Warned that his mother, already in trouble and on probation, would go to jail for contributing to the delinquency of a minor if he continued, LaRance quickly agreed to forego that lucrative occupation so as not to jeopardize her.

Then in 1945, when he was fourteen, his teachers noted that he seemed to have a cold all the time and was losing weight noticeably. He was sent to the county clinic, given vitamins. His work permit to sell papers was revoked. Instead he was given a job in the high school cafeteria where he was assured at least one substantial meal a day. After that it was noted that he gained a pound a week.

He was rated high as a worker and it was the cafeteria job he put down on his army application as his pre-enlistment work experience.

Matters at home got no better. It is a tribute to the Santa Barbara police that when LaRance did not know what to do to protect his sisters from the frightening scenes at home he brought them to the police station for refuge.

"Today," said Dr. Elmott, "we have progressed in psychological treatment with the Mental Hygiene Clinic and the family service agency at Neighborhood House and we could have worked more intensively with the mother."

But in that day it was inevitable that Laura Mae would finally go to the county jail and serve a sentence for violating probation. When that happened LaRance's sisters were put in foster homes.

"We kept LaRance at Juvenile Hall," said John B. Clark, senior probation officer. "It's hard as the dickens to find a foster home for a teenage Negro boy."

Clark remembers LaRance as a "quiet, personable boy," never a problem and well liked by the other youngsters as well as the staff.

LaRance stayed at Juvenile Hall, free to come and go because he had no offense charged against him. He lived there for several periods while he went to high school.

Perhaps Santa Barbara's best try at helping him was through its Boys' Club. Now in a fine new home with a fully equipped gymnasium of its own near the high school, the Boys' Club in LaRance's day was working on a shoestring. Even so, from the age of eleven on LaRance had his happiest times there and if he could have stayed longer at the club "he might have made it," the director, Gordon J. Wormal, believes.

Boys of all social and financial levels participate in the club and there are no distinctions of race or color. LaRance found his best friend and rival there, Angelo Juarez. Angelo and he both made the try for the chin-up championship, but, as young LaRance shot toward the six foot three he was to reach, he grew stronger than Angelo and was able to chin himself fifty-five times, as against forty-eight for his friend.

Although at high school LaRance was definitely considered a follower rather than a leader, at the summer camp sessions of the Boys' Club he was singled out as one of the junior leaders and was looked up to with admiration and devotion by the younger boys.

His sister Anita was sure that the only real happiness her brother ever had was in the Boys' Club.

"LaRance was real sensitive," she said. "He would cry in

a minute over something nobody else would notice. It's hard on a boy to see his mother pushed this way and that. A man's different than a woman, I guess. He takes things like that harder.

"He didn't really know what he wanted to do. When he was little, it was an acrobat. But he was always drawing pictures of houses—the houses he was going to get for Mother—and I guess maybe he would have liked to be an architect.

"He might never have gotten in that prison camp if it hadn't been for my stepfather. LaRance changed his mind after he applied the first time. He was underage so Mother would have to sign. He told her he didn't want to go any more, but my stepfather made her sign. He said, 'then we'll be rid of him.'

"He never had any trouble with the other kids because of his color. Most of his friends were outside his own race. He had a good sense of humor and was the joy of the crowd."

LaRance went into battle with the 2nd Division early in the fall of 1950, the first year of the war. He was in on the race to the Yalu River on the Manchurian border at the time when General Douglas MacArthur was counting on getting American soldiers "home by Christmas." Sullivan was one of the first to be captured in the overwhelming and unexpected Chinese offensive that delayed the homecoming for three years. He was reported missing on November 25, 1950. In prison camp he soon developed tuberculosis because of the privations and the physical conditions of those early months of imprisonment.

On the Chinese radio LaRance said that Anita would understand "why I am doing this."

In a way Anita does understand and yet—

"It's something hard to understand," she said, "unless they really tell it to you themselves."

Mrs. Frost, his step-grandmother, understands even less.

"This is like to kill me," Mrs. Frost says, rocking and moaning as she thinks of her cute little guy. "Never heard of Communism until this war. Never heard of Korea. They'll make a slave out of him."

Mrs. Frost has a letter from LaRance written in November of 1952, two years after his capture.

"It sounds like him, and then again it don't," Mrs. Frost told me. "He called me Mama, like he always did, but then he says all this other."

What he wrote that puzzled Mrs. Frost was this:

I came to realize since I became a prisoner of war exactly what I am fighting for. I have come to realize that the war is not being fought for the common people like you and I, but for a handful of Wall streets. It really came as a surprise to me when I looked at my country from the outside.

Since my capture I have been in a prisoner of war hospital and I have been treated very well. It is surprising how well I have been treated because I was of the belief when I first got captured that I would be killed. But as you can see, Mama, I am still alive, thanks to the CPV (Chinese People's Volunteers).

I am hoping with all my heart that all you folks will stay in the mood for peace. Maybe soon all the boys will be back home. One thing for sure, Mama, if everyone gets in the move for peace, some day the common people will win.

Keep sweet and pray for us all.

Your loving grandson,

No one knows if LaRance had yet heard the shocking news about his mother, though by then he could have.

The Ventura *Star Press* summarized it starkly in a news story of August 17, 1951:

Enrique Maytorena, forty-eight, went to state prison today to serve a ten-year sentence for second-degree murder in the fatal beating of Mrs. Laura Mae Moten, in a hotel room in nearby Oxnard, a month ago. He told police he had beaten her as punishment for trying to steal his wallet.

Pierre Moten, LaRance's stepfather, had already died earlier that month in a truck accident at a summer resort.

Meanwhile LaRance's own father, a furniture warehouseman who now lives in Omaha with his second wife, and who hasn't seen his son since he was a child, is more puzzled than anyone.

"I'll never believe it," he said. "It couldn't be true. Why, he didn't have a hard time. He never knew segregation. He didn't live in the South."

Cpl. Scott Leonard Rush

of Akron, O.

born August 18, 1932

enlisted August 19, 1949

3rd Division

captured November 26, 1950

Catholic

8th grade

low I.Q.

The Army Reported:

> *According to returned prisoners of war, Rush was a member of the "Kremlin Club" and was a devoted student of Communism. As a reward for his efforts to convert fellow prisoners, he was appointed a librarian and received better food and medical care than prisoners who resisted Communism.*

SCOTT LEONARD RUSH was a slight, delicate boy with wide eyes and a baby face when he enlisted in the army in 1949, the day after his seventeenth birthday. When he headed for China in January of 1954, still slight and delicate, he was only twenty-two, no longer wide-eyed, no longer baby-faced, no longer a boy.

His face was lined and weary, pared to a hollowness about chin and cheeks, his eyelids sagged, his mouth was twisted and turned down at the corners, his frail, small frame cramped like that of an old man.

The chances are that if Leonard, or Peewee, as he was variously known, had waited until his eighteenth birthday the army wouldn't have taken him at all, with a war on. He wasn't exactly army material. Small, only five foot two, Leonard was a "slow learner" who had been considered in need of clinical help for his emotional difficulties at the special public school he attended.

That is the Miller Occupational School in Akron, where despite few facilities and a lean budget, small miracles are being worked with boys who have difficulty in keeping up with their classmates. The school is still feeling its way in its attempt to solve the problems of the child who can't seem to learn to read—to find ways of teaching him or, failing that, to teach him other skills that will make it possible for him to take his place in the world.

They haven't found all the answers yet and Leonard Rush

was one of the school's first students. There was no possibility of getting him the expensive help he needed.

Leonard's parents are both alive and there has been no divorce in the family. Yet, rightly or wrongly, he felt unwanted. This sense of not belonging was increased when he was fifteen and his parents moved away from Akron, leaving Leonard and his brother Richard behind. Richard was put in a Catholic boarding school. Leonard lived in a basement room and earned his way through school working as a dishwasher at a local hotel.

At the Mayflower Hotel the kitchen staff called him "about as quiet a kid as you'd ever find; speak to him and he'd smile a little but he'd hardly ever say a word."

Neighbors in Akron called him a "nice lad" who didn't play much but who worked hard after school, selling papers on downtown street corners, and caddying before he got the dishwashing job, a boy with no close pals, who had never had a girl.

At the Miller School his skills were developed and latent leadership qualities brought out. He became foreman of the metal shop and showed a strong sense of responsibility, according to the principal, Esmond Thomas. There he thrived and expressed himself and was not the withdrawn boy he remained outside of the school atmosphere.

The teachers and the principal were aware of deep-lying personal maladjustments but the school's budget could not include such expensive items as individual psychological and clinical therapy.

I visited the classes at the Miller School. Boys who have gone through the elementary grades without learning to read well enough to tackle regular high school work go there instead of to high school.

Because, to most of them, books represent the failure that

has dogged them through their school years, no books at all are brought out in the beginning classes. The boys grow plants, breed hamsters, play games, work with their hands in an atmosphere where they are not the class "dummies." Once they begin to relax and trust their teacher, reading matter is brought out tentatively, perhaps in the form of an automobile brochure or a pamphlet on woodworking.

Some respond swiftly and go from the second to the sixth grade in reading ability in a year. For those that still can't master book learning, there is the chance to stay in school until they are eighteen and learn a trade.

Other boys who enlisted with Leonard from the Miller School, and who escaped capture, distinguished themselves in Korea and came back to establish a place for themselves in the community. Among the school's small alumni group are a minister, a builder and a store owner. Leonard too might have been able to find his place, those who knew him felt, if circumstances had not led him to a Korean prison camp.

Leonard graduated from the school in June of 1949 and went to Marietta, O., where his parents were now living. Two months later he enlisted in the army and became a combat photographer in the 3rd Division.

He was only in battle a few days before he was captured. The 3rd Division landed in Korea early in November and got into the front lines just in time to be hit by the waves of fresh Chinese troops that turned what seemed to be victory into a rout.

He was captured on November 26, 1950, but it was a long time before his family knew that he was captured. His first letter, when it finally came through, said:

"I am alive and safe. I sure wish the war was over so we could get to come home. Give my love to all and pray for me so I will come home."

Fellow prisoners were surprised to find that Peewee was one of those who had agreed to stay with the Chinese Reds. He had been "mildly progressive," but hardly more than the general run who didn't see any point in "trying to be a hero" when all you got for your heroism were beatings and frozen feet.

I went to Marietta to see his parents. His father answered my ring. When I told him my mission he said grimly:

"I'm not going to say a thing."

"Perhaps Mrs. Rush . . ."

"You aren't even going to see Mrs. Rush," he said and slammed the door.

Rush had consistently refused to talk to reporters after the news was announced that Leonard was one of the twenty-one but Mrs. Rush had been interviewed and photographed with a hand-tinted picture of her boy when the news was first announced. A tiny, dark-haired woman—she is four foot ten —she had spoken of Leonard's "wonderful personality."

"When Sonny was reported missing in action, I knew that he was alive," she told reporters. "And now I know he's coming home. Just as I know he's not turned Communist. It isn't something that you can explain. It's something that you feel deep in your heart."

But Sonny isn't coming home. Before he left for the interior of China he told correspondents that the decision to stay with the Reds was "my own, there was no intimidation or attempt to persuade me to stay back. The Chinese tried many times to get me to come back, but I am determined to fight for peace and this is the only place where I will have the freedom to do it."

Sonny isn't coming home. But that pathetically frail, old before his time, figure who marched with the twenty-one behind the Iron Curtain isn't Sonny, either.

Pfc. Otho G. Bell

of Hillsboro, Miss.

born January 23, 1931

enlisted January 29, 1949

2nd Division

captured November 30, 1950

Protestant

8th grade

low I.Q.

The Army Reported:

According to returned prisoners of war, Bell voluntarily attended Communist indoctrination meetings and assisted the Communists in their efforts to get other prisoners to accept Communism. He made propaganda recordings and signed peace petitions. For his willing efforts, he was made a mail orderly.

OTHO BELL was twenty-three on January 23, 1954, the day
his native land receded from him forever, the last day when he
could change his mind and go back to his wife and the daughter he had never seen, the farm in Mississippi where he had
been raised.

Otho's mother was twenty-three the day she died, January
23, 1931—the day he was born—and Otho had grown up feeling that he had "killed his mother" to the point where he got
the idea he himself would die on his twenty-third birthday.

It isn't necessary to presume that Otho's "decision" to stay
with his Red jailers was a decision to die so far as home and
family and country were concerned. Otho had other strikes
against him too.

He had not been educated, as one teacher put it, "to the
point where he would be a good citizen of a democracy or
would be capable of judging what the Reds told him."

On the other hand, he had learned to do what he was told—
and no backtalk.

"I could always scare him into anything," his father, Elbert
A. Bell, said, "and if I had the chance I could have scared him
into coming back home."

But it was the Chinese Communists, not Otho's father, who
had the chance to scare him into doing what they wanted him
to do—and they succeeded well enough so that Otho, though
the only one of the twenty-one with a wife and child, went
behind the Iron Curtain with the others.

Claude Batchelor, originally one of the group, who broke for freedom at the last moment to rejoin his Japanese wife, told Otho's wife, Jewell Bell, that her husband had been convinced by the Chinese that she and their daughter Paula would be able to join him in China.

When I talked to her in Olympia, Wash., where she was supporting herself by taking care of six young children whose parents had gone to Alaska, I asked Mrs. Bell if she would be willing to go to Otho if arrangements could be made.

"If I were alone, I would go to him anywhere," she said, her eyes filling with tears, "just so he would be sure that someone loved him. But I could not do that to Paula."

Despite his mother's youth when she died at his birth, Otho was her fifth child. His father remarried when Otho was seven months old and there were six more children by this marriage.

"He was just the same as my own, I had him so young," the second Mrs. Bell told me. "He was just as much mine as the next one who's only a year and a half younger. Seems like I thought more of him at times than the others."

But Otho knew that his own mother had died when he was born. Away from home he brooded over it and felt that he was less favored than his younger half brothers and sisters. In a way it was true. Times were a little easier as the younger children came along. The 160 acres of sandy soil which his father was making into a farm began to pay off and the younger ones had things that Otho had had to do without. He was too young to understand the reasons.

The farm is a few miles down back roads from Hillsboro, Miss., a hamlet consisting of two general stores, a tiny post office, a filling station and a feed store. The family is old Mississippi stock on both sides and has lived in the area for some generations.

Otho G. Bell

The farmhouse has always been too small for the burgeoning Bell family and there are beds in every room. Mrs. Bell talked to me in the parlor where there were framed pictures of Otho and of his wife and daughter. Small and round-faced, her hair pulled into a knot at the back of her head, her housedress covered with a big white apron, Mrs. Bell sat with her hands clasped in her lap most of the time that we talked.

"Otho was a good little boy," Mrs. Bell told me. "He didn't fight with the other children—he got along too good with them. Most of the time he did what he was told but if you did have to switch him he would sit down and cry a little and then go out and play."

He didn't get into fights with the other children, "he got along too good," he did "what he was told" and he was "patient" if he couldn't get what he wanted.

Otho's father has pushed himself to the limit to put the farm on a paying basis and it finally is. The family now has a tractor, a shiny new car, an enormous chicken house and twenty-three head of cattle.

Bell worked hard and expected his boys to do likewise; he expected them to come a-running when he called them and they did—Otho in particular.

"He was a real good worker," his father says of him. "He was one of the best workers I ever saw. He was strong and healthy. I always taught my children to work. If boys don't work they do something else like stealing or robbing banks. He was easy to manage. I could just scare him into doing anything I wanted him to do."

Otho was a "good little boy," everybody who knew him agrees, who may have been "mischievous on occasion," but never got into fights, never caused anybody any trouble.

Growing up, he worked hard and played hard, picking cotton in the fields, hunting for possum and squirrel in the woods, fishing the streams for cat and trout. He didn't like school and didn't do well there. He spent three years in the eighth grade. The third year he was kept company by a half brother, on his second try, and a half sister on her first.

His teachers liked him. One, Mrs. Olive Gatewood, was particularly fond of him and he returned her affection. Before he went overseas he brought her a book, *The Case of the Backward Mule,* and he wrote her a letter from prison camp.

"I can still see him," Mrs. Gatewood said, "with his shoes unshined and his shirttail hanging out. He had a good sense of humor if it did run to practical jokes. But he would rather hunt possum nights than go to school days."

When Otho was making one of his tries at the eighth grade, his class was transferred to the new Consolidated School at the county seat, Forest, a booming lumber and chicken-processing center.

If he hadn't liked school before, he really hated it now. The town children were "uppity" to the country school transfers and Otho's family got him into another country school district where he got his diploma finally, complete with cap and gown.

Otho didn't go on to high school. He was pleased to be out of the eighth grade at last and he was through with school. But he was restless. He wanted a car. He wanted to be a truck driver with a big trailer truck. He wanted to be a cop. He settled for an enlistment in the army.

With another local boy he ran off across the river to Louisiana and enlisted a few days after his seventeenth birthday. He lied about his age and was accepted. He didn't take much to army life and after a few months he wrote his father begging him to get him out.

"He was glad to get his pa's help to get him out," Mrs.

Bell told me, "though he hadn't got his signature to get him in. He had a little spree with a rattletrap car he bought on his army pay. And then he was back in again, because they kept ding-donging at him about the other boy staying in even if he was underage too. He didn't want anybody to think he was chicken."

His second enlistment was a few days after his eighteenth birthday in January, 1949. He didn't like army life any better than he had before. He phoned home—collect—so often that the bills began to worry his father. He was always writing for money to come home on weekend leave and when he came home he never wanted to go back. Three times he overstayed and was convicted by courtmartial of being AWOL. He was fined a total of $125 and sentenced to seventy-seven days of hard labor for his offenses.

Then he was sent to Fort Lewis, Wash., near Seattle where he met his future wife. Jewell and he were married only a few months before the Korean war started. The 2nd Division was alerted for Korea early in July and landed at Pusan early in August. Paula was born just before he was captured in November of 1950.

"He was real good to me," Jewell told me, "he wouldn't let me do any heavy work after we knew the baby was coming. After he got overseas he wrote me five letters a week even if it was only a line."

The letters which had come during all the days of the early defeats in the beginning of the war, through the victory march up to the Yalu River, stopped for a long while after he was captured in that November rout which broke up the 2nd Division.

Until the peace conference started, no letters came out of North Korean prison camps, and families knew only that their boys were missing.

When his letters started coming again they weren't quite the same. They asked his wife to work for peace and had the usual line about how the North Koreans and the Chinese were not to blame for the war—"I would be home now if the Americans would stop fighting."

His family too got letters like these, as well as others talking about how anxious he was to get home, how much he missed his mother's chocolate cake and banana pudding. He asked how his hunting dog Old Jute was getting on and about his Uncle Joe with whom he used to go hunting.

When the news came that Otho was one of the group that would refuse repatriation, Jewell brought their little daughter down to Mississippi to visit the Bells. Later she went to Washington with Aaron Wilson's family to see if she could get to Korea and talk to Otho.

The Bells, like the other families, made a recording pleading with their boy to come home.

"Just imagine, son," his father said, "that I have my arms around you. Imagine that I am right there by you, kissing you on the cheek. We all want you home, son. I can guarantee you will not be harmed. Tell the Indians that you want to come home and they will let you."

Like the other recordings that were made by families and friends, this one was never heard by Otho.

The elder Bell tried to get permission, then, to go over to Korea and see his son in person. The local American Legion Post campaigned to raise the passage money. But the Defense Department refused to let him go.

When Edward Dickenson left the compound early in October and came home to his family in the hill country of Virginia, the Bells trekked up to Cracker's Neck to see him.

They were able only to talk to his parents and did not get much consolation from their visit.

Nor did Otho's wife get much consolation from her correspondence with Claude Batchelor, the other G.I. who escaped.

Jewell wrote to Batchelor asking him about Otho and if it were true that the twenty-one had been doped.

In his answer he said he was sorry to have to say that "we were duped rather than doped."

"Otho's chief reason for staying behind," he wrote on January 21, 1954, in the first of two letters to his friend's wife, "was not so much from political reasons as from fear, though he had done nothing to be afraid of.

"Bell is very much confused over the political situation and before I left I'm sure he was thinking whether he was doing right or not. He used to talk to me occasionally and I tried in an indirect way to discourage him from staying. I thought perhaps when I left a few others would have followed. However Radio Peiping says I am undergoing third-degree methods of torture to extract information and atrocity stories from me, which is an outright lie."

He told her that Otho had twice been in the hospital at Panmunjom, "which is completely staffed by Chinese and North Koreans," once with a sprained back and once when he was "having some trouble with his wisdom teeth."

Otho's fear was "Communist-instilled," Batchelor wrote, "and partly comes from G.I.'s who were prisoners with him. You see, he, like myself, was one of those prisoners of war who, wanting to do good for the American people, fell for a bit of the Chinese propaganda and became what was known as progressives. . . . Other G.I.'s started labeling them rats, informers, traitors, etc., when actually they were under the impression that what they were doing was right. Several rumors went around camp about Bell (false, as I have found out) that there was a circular being circulated in the army saying, 'Don't be a Bell' and listing several things he was alleged to have done. I have checked on that and found it to be false but Otho doesn't or can't know about it. So with these things weighing on the fellow's mind, it makes it hard for him to come home."

He warned Otho's wife not to "get your hopes all built up because the possibility exists that he will not come home, in fact, very likely. I warn you only so that it will not be too much of a letdown should we fail."

In his second letter written on February 2, after Otho had gone behind the Iron Curtain with the rest, Batchelor told Mrs. Bell how sorry he was that the letters he had sent Otho weren't delivered to him and hadn't changed his mind.

"These things may be a little hard for you to comprehend especially when I tell you that Otho had the greatest love for you and Paula," Batchelor wrote. "I have the deepest sympathy for you and especially for Paula. Bell was a good friend of mine and he told me many things about you and the child he had never seen. We often talked intimately about our wives. We were the only two in camp who were married and it bound us together."

He told her that he thought she could still write to Otho through the Chinese People's Committee for World Peace but warned her to be "prepared for almost nothing but Communist propaganda. . . . Please don't make the mistake I did. Turn your efforts to educating young Paula to learn what it is to live in a free country where she can say and do as she likes without fear. Teach her to love and respect people of all races and to govern her life according to humanitarian principles. She has never seen her father. She doesn't have to know until she is old enough to understand.

"Do not let this incident destroy you as it would have

done my wife. She was already contemplating suicide when I came home.

"Life is still ahead of you. You are young and you have a long life ahead of you in our free America. More than yourself you have a great obligation resting on your shoulders. Young Paula's father is gone. What would she do without her mother? These things you must think about and gather courage to go through life with a proud head. Proud that you are a good American who is fulfilling an obligation to life. There are people who will not understand. A few will point and say bad things. But there are many, many more who will point and say this woman has courage. The bad types are only a few. The good are many. You have absolutely nothing to worry about.

"Take my advice, Mrs. Bell. Find Paula a new father, one she can love and respect, a man of courage who will shelter her as his own. Give her a chance to know the love of a father so she doesn't get discouraged by a lot she doesn't understand."

Jewell Bell has no intention of taking this last advice. Just before I visited her, she had received a letter from her husband—one of the rare messages received by any of the families of the twenty-one. He asked if she and Paula still loved him and added, "I am wondering if you are planning to marry someone else or still want to be my wife."

Talking to me in the living room of her temporary home, with the children she was caring for and Paula romping up and down it, the tears came to her eyes as she told me that she had written Otho that he would always be her husband and that Paula prays for him every night.

She is under a doctor's care for the nervous tension that has never left her since the day she heard Otho was going to stay with the Chinese Communists. It shows in her eyes and in her face. But it is gone when she speaks to the children, her own Paula as well as the six under her care. Her response to them is wholehearted and they all love her devotedly.

One of the boys guided me to a drugstore where I could buy flashbulbs for my camera.

"Do you miss your father and mother much?" I asked him.

"Gee, I guess so," he answered, "sure, but gee, we sure like Jewell. She's the only baby sitter we ever had that we liked. That's why Mom got her to come and stay with us while they went away."

But life stretches bleakly ahead for Paula and her mother. The youngster can pick her father out of the group pictures taken of the twenty-one before they left for China and she points proudly to a cabinet photograph of him and says:

"That's my daddy."

She doesn't understand why he doesn't come home, why she doesn't have a daddy who is there in person like the other children she knows. Or why she can't have the wagon she wants so much—like the one her playmates have. "My daddy will get one for me, when he comes home," she keeps saying belligerently. As yet she is too young to understand, but the time will come when she will have to know her father's story.

Cpl. Albert C. Belhomme

of Ashland, Pa.

born in Antwerp, Belgium, November 7, 1928

enlisted November 6, 1948

2nd Division

captured November 30, 1950

Catholic

European education

high I.Q.

The Army Reported:

According to returned prisoners of war, he wrote articles for the Communist publication Toward Truth and Peace *and created slogans for Communist posters displayed in camp. He was a member of the "Kremlin Club" which was devoted to special study of Communist ideology and to discussions of Communism in the international situation. Belhomme was a leader of a Communist study group and was used as a liaison man between prisoners and Communist camp authorities.*

In MANY WAYS the case of Albert Belhomme is a curious paradox. Born in Belgium and brought here by his mother when she married an American G.I., Albert had little time to put down roots in his adopted country before he was made prisoner by the Chinese Reds.

Conversely, as a foreigner, he was the only one of the twenty-one who chose to stay with their Red captors who had previously chosen to be an American. He had taken out his first papers; had joined the army, actually, to speed up the process of becoming a citizen.

In an interview before he left Panmunjom to go behind the Iron Curtain, Belhomme pointed out that he had spent five years of his life "under Hitler's occupation" and that he had no wish to go back to more of the same which he was now certain would be his lot in America.

As a refugee from Europe, Albert had seemed to appreciate the democratic principles of his adopted country to a greater degree than boys who had grown up knowing nothing else. Still he was not immune to the idea that what had happened in Europe could happen in America.

Alone of the twenty-one, he had had real contact with Communism and Communists, and might be supposed to have acquired some sophistication as to their goals and methods. But he knew Communists only as staunch members of the Underground, allies in the fight against Hitler at a time when their plans and their goals were veiled under the guise of the United Front—and he was hardly more than a child.

When Albert was born in Antwerp, Belgium, in 1928, peace and prosperity began to seem like established institutions. Yet there was a shadow across Albert's life before he was scarcely able to talk.

"Our daddy was mean to him," his mother, Marcella Belhomme Seifert, put it. "He slapped him around. That's why we separated."

The child had such a severe case of asthma that he spent most of the years between the ages of two and five in a sanitarium. He recovered sufficiently to go to the parish school where he soon became the most brilliant student.

"The priest said he studied too much," Mrs. Seifert said. "He could learn to speak any language he wanted to."

Albert was eleven when the war came. He was twelve when his father was killed. He was thirteen when he beat his way to Berlin to find his mother who had been put in a slave labor camp there. He stayed there with her and was with her when she met an American G.I., Theodore L. Seifert of Ashland, Pa.

"Albert liked Ted from the beginning," Mrs. Seifert said. "He was happy when we told him we were going to be married, asked if he could start calling him Dad from then on."

Because of Albert, there were some complications about the two coming into this country but they were allowed entry in 1946 when Albert was eighteen. He took out his first citizenship papers but wasn't able to get a regular job even though he had become an expert drill press operator in Germany.

For a time he attended occasional classes at Ashland High School with some of his friends, to pick up English. There is a story current in the town that he resented "being used as an assistant teacher" because his German accent was so good, and stopped going to class on that account. However, school records do not show that he was ever an enrolled student and the German teacher does not remember him even visiting in class.

He tried to get in the navy, was turned down for flat feet, and finally enlisted in the army in November of 1948. In the meantime he had made himself a part of the community in two short years, with a host of friends.

One of his friends remembered him as "quieter than the average and brighter than the average; he picked up English in a few months and spoke it flawlessly."

Another spoke of how he had helped the students he knew with both German and French and quickly became one of the gang.

"He wouldn't talk about his experiences in the war," another one said. "I guess they must have been pretty bad. And there were times when I thought he wasn't very stable. He certainly hadn't had a stable life."

He was handy around the house, made bookcases out of crates, painted and fixed things up generally, his mother said. He and his stepfather, a railroad worker, got along fine. "He would do anything for his dad."

Once in the army he passed all the tests for officers' training but one: he had not yet gotten his citizenship. After basic training he was sent over to Germany for three months, recalled and sent to Seattle, then to Korea with the 2nd Division.

His mother remembers how proud he was of his uniform when he was home on leave and how he changed his suntans three times a day so as to always look neat and fresh.

The Chinese Reds captured Albert on November 25, 1950. He was held in four different camps, acting as liaison man between prisoners and their captors. He was not accused of being an informer.

Of all the twenty-one, Belhomme is undoubtedly the Chinese Reds' prize catch, useful in more ways than just as a propaganda gesture. His phenomenal ability with languages showed up when he learned Korean and Chinese to the point where he "could speak like a native." In addition he knew Flemish, Dutch, French, German and English and could pass as a native in any of these languages.

Mrs. Seifert, a slight, pleasant-faced woman who does day work, is as puzzled as any of the other mothers over her son's refusal to come back.

"He loved this country," she told me. "He didn't want to go back to Belgium. And he had about $6,000 coming to him."

His letters did not hint at any intention of staying with the Chinese Reds. His last letter, sent in May of 1953, said, "Mom, for God's sake, pray that the truce talks go through and I can come home; we'll have a gay time."

Earlier he had written:

Americans should not feel too badly toward the pros because these boys had been under some awful conditions in the enemy prison camps.

This was in April when progressives were a large part of the group of wounded prisoners exchanged under special terms, in "Operation Little Switch."

Even when it was all over and her son had gone behind the Iron Curtain, Mrs. Seifert had not given up hope.

"They'll come back, one by one, when they see what's going on in Russia. I can't understand Albert or those boys."

Now she's not so sure they'll be able to come back—even one by one. She has had no word from Albert since that January day they started for the interior of China.

Pfc. Aaron P. Wilson

of Urania, La.

born July 28, 1932

enlisted March, 1950

7th Division

captured November 30, 1950

Baptist

8th grade

low I.Q.

The Army Reported:

According to returned prisoners of war, Wilson performed special duties for the Chinese Communists, circulating peace petitions, making recordings for Communist propaganda broadcasts, participated in Communist study group meetings and tried to win converts to Communism. His rewards included more and better food and a greater degree of freedom than that given other prisoners.

"**R**EMEMBER BEFORE THE WAR when you got lost one day while hunting and we brought you out of the woods? Well, we still feel the same way, only this time we are trying to bring you out of the woods of Communism."

These words were addressed to Aaron P. Wilson of Urania, La., by Sheriff Floyd of LaSalle Parish. They were part of a recorded plea sent to him while he was in the neutral zone at Panmunjom and could still change his mind about refusing to come back to his country.

It is doubtful if Aaron ever heard Sheriff Floyd's plea, or the voices of his parents and favorite sister begging him to come home. It is doubtful if it would have made any difference if he had. Aaron's family, with some reason, believe their boy is one of three who, South Koreans said, wanted to come back but were "scared."

"He was a humble boy who never sassed me in his life," says his mother, Mrs. Henry B. Wilson. "When he was whipped he would stand up like a humble little dog and take his punishment."

"Not another boy in that town would've got lost in those woods and had to be led out," said a former resident of Urania. "Without you could go in and lead him out of that Communist camp, there was no chance he'd come out of there either."

"He was a lonely kid, quiet, not as bright as he should

be," said a neighbor. "He stayed to himself, played to himself, never did what the other kids did; never even played ball."

"My brother couldn't have written those letters," said his sister Myrtle, of the Communist propaganda he wrote home. "He was too dumb to write like that. Why, when he went in the Army he was seventeen and still in the eighth grade."

"Aaron was afraid he would be prosecuted if he came home" was the word sent to his family by Claude Batchelor, the prisoner of war who slipped out of the compound just before the deadline. "But he hasn't anything to fear. A lot of other prisoners informed on their buddies. But Aaron was straight and never did anything like that."

Nor does the army accuse him, as it does twelve of the twenty-one, of being an informer.

Whether he was scared or stupid, or both, whether he fell for the Communist line, or the Communist lures, Aaron went behind the Iron Curtain January 28, 1954, with the twenty-one.

This was not the first time that Aaron's family had had to get used to the idea of doing without him. He was reported dead rather than missing in the fall of 1950 and it wasn't until 1952 that it was established that he was alive and a prisoner. In the meantime the army paid his war insurance.

And he almost died at birth, as the result of a forceps injury. For two weeks he hovered between life and death.

"Then he had the three months' colic," Mrs. Wilson remembered. "And a fever so bad we had to hold him in a pan of water to cool him off."

Aaron survived that and an emergency appendectomy before he was two. From then on there is no record of illness until in his teens when he ruptured himself helping build a barn for the Baptist church. He had to wear a support, his sister said, and "we wouldn't let him tussle around no more."

Oldest and only boy for thirteen years, Aaron was born the second summer of the depression in a company house in the company-owned lumber town of Urania, deep in the Piney Woods section of Louisiana. His father has always worked for the Urania Lumber Company—when there was work— and his highest wage had been seventy-five cents an hour. It was much less than that when Aaron was growing up. A cow, a pig and a vegetable garden are necessities for most of the residents in Urania if their families are to have enough to eat. The houses are heated with wood stoves and until recently all cooking was done on wood stoves. Some residents boast that it's an "all-white town, not a nigger in ten miles."

It's also a town where the word is passed around quickly that a stranger is around. I asked directions to the Wilson place and after two or three wrong turns finally found it. There was no one home. But before I could decide whether to wait or leave, a slick blue car drove up. Mrs. Wilson was at the wheel. She'd heard that someone was asking for her.

The Wilsons had eight children; six survive. The baby, Glenda Joyce, two, was born while Aaron was in prison camp and he has never seen her. Closest to him in age and affection is Myrtle Elaine, twenty, now married to airman Robert W. Rogers and living near the air base at Alexandria, La.

"Aaron was the favorite of all of us," Myrtle told me. "He was our pet. I remember the first day he went to school. He was six in July, but I wasn't old enough yet. We slept together. That morning he shook me and said, 'Wake up sister and kiss me goodbye.' "

If Aaron acted as though going to school was like setting out on a long journey, he wasn't far wrong. For him, school was a strange, unhappy place and he never got accustomed to it, even though he spent two years in nearly every grade.

His teachers felt he did as well as he could, but that he was apathetic to teaching, passing most of his days dreaming and looking out the window. He was stubborn and docile by turns, "you couldn't tell whether or not he was a good loser— he just accepted it."

His classmates didn't bully him or pick on him—"they didn't pay that much attention to him." Most of his school days he was bigger and older than the rest of his classmates, but he attempted neither to lead them or to bully them on that account.

"He just spent most of his time by himself," one teacher said. "He would look up at you from under those eyebrows of his and seem to say, 'Try to get at me, try to make me happy.' But the teachers didn't get any closer to him than the children did."

"I hit him with a board once," another teacher told me (corporal punishment is allowed in Louisiana schools), "though he didn't usually need disciplining, and it really did hurt me worse than it did him. He just stood there and took it."

Myrtle soon passed him in school and became in effect a second mother and an older brother to him.

"I felt sorry for him because he wouldn't take up for himself," she told me as we talked in her one-room apartment in a made-over frame house in Alexandria. "He'd take more than I ever would. He never fought but once in his life. He'd let anybody take his things and they'd never bring them back. I took up for him when he wouldn't take up for himself."

After he hurt himself working on the church barn, Myrtle "didn't like him to tussle around with others." When his

bike needed repair, she let him "have all the parts off mine."
When she went away he missed her.

"I remember one time I went off to Columbia to visit
and I wasn't there but a few days when Aaron showed up.
He thumbed a ride. He told me Mother wanted me to come
home. But she hadn't at all, he just wanted me home."

Myrtle felt that while her brother was quiet with new
people, he was on the whole "too friendly." Myrtle didn't
think her parents had been too hard on Aaron.

"Maybe they were too easy on us. If we couldn't get something from daddy, we would go to Mother and get it. We
always had our own way in the end. I know Mother worried
when he stayed out late. She'd be there in front of the heater
waiting for him."

But Mrs. Wilson felt they had been neither too hard nor
too easy on their son. "He was a good boy; he didn't need
many whippings; he was a humble child; he never drank in
his life; the only thing he ever defied me on was cigarettes;
he wanted to smoke and I finally let him."

Aaron liked to hunt and his life's ambition was to live on
a farm. He loved horses and western movies, comic books,
and to strum on "the old guitar." He didn't take good care of
his own things but his sister tried to do it for him. "Oh,
sometimes he'd take a smart spell." He was good at changing a flat or remaking a bike out of two old ones. He drew
the water for his mother and worked at odd jobs mowing
yards, "but only when he felt like it."

His sister said he pestered his father for two years to sign
his recruitment papers; his mother believed that "the re-
cruiter down to Olla" was responsible for his enlisting.

At any rate, he went in on March 13, 1950, while he was
still seventeen, a few months before the Korean conflict

started. He had his last leave that July, after the war had started, and his sister said she had never seen him so upset.

"I hate to leave Mother and daddy but I got to go," he told her. "But I want them to leave me, I don't want to leave them. Get them to go away before we pull out."

And that was the last time that Aaron and his family have seen each other. He was sent to Korea immediately—he had had fourteen weeks of basic training—and he was reported killed in the rout at the end of November, that year.

With the insurance money, the family bought the new car and the farm up in northern Louisiana which Aaron had always wanted. Aaron's father told him about the farm in the recording they made; about the sixty bales of cotton and the good corn that had been harvested by the people he had farming it and added, "I will give you a car when you come home."

In 1952, word came through that Aaron was on a list of prisoners given out by the Communists and they began to get letters from him. They were strange letters for Aaron to write.

"He didn't know nothing about Communism," Myrtle says. "Any more than I did—or any more than I do now for that matter."

His mother had an idea he might not be coming home when his letters stopped coming after April of 1953.

"I talked to a lot of other returnees and they told us about those classes where they taught the boys Communist politics," Mrs. Wilson said. "And when his name was not on the list of freed prisoners, we had an idea he might be thinking about staying. But that is not his will. He is not that kind of a boy."

The Wilsons called on Senator Russell Long of Louisiana to help get Aaron back. They wrote to Representative Passman, to Senator McCarthy, to President Eisenhower and even to an Indian guard with the Neutral Nations Repatriation Commission whose name they saw in a newspaper.

They asked the guard to give Aaron their telephone number—they had had a phone installed since getting the insurance money—and ask him to call them.

They asked Eisenhower to let them go over and see Aaron.

"I got a letter from the President telling me that, according to the armistice agreement, parents are not allowed to see their sons in the Communist camp," Mrs. Wilson said. "I don't think that's fair. If the mothers and fathers of those boys could see them and talk to them they would all come home."

Myrtle went to Washington with the wife and mother of another prisoner of war, Otho Bell, and tried to get a passport to get to Tokyo herself. In the meantime she gave Mrs. Portia Howe (who got as far as Japan in trying to see her son, Richard Tenneson) a letter for Aaron. That letter he did receive. It read:

Hi Aaron: I am coming to Japan in hopes that I can see you. I'll send you another message when I arrive in Japan. Please ask permission to see me. Mom and Dad are not able to make the trip because of bad health. Please do as I say just once as I want to see you once again. I'm praying for you.

Love,
Myrtle Elaine

To this she got a reply, but "it is not my brother talking at all," she said after she read it. "My brother was too dumb to write a letter like that. Someone addressed it, signed it Bud, and filled in the middle."

Aaron's letter read in part:

Aaron P. Wilson

It is most surprising to hear that you are being allowed
to come to Japan. I was wondering who is supporting you in
this unexpected trip and I bet you had to go through quite
a bit of red tape in order to get your passport, etc.

It's a wonder the government is allowing you to come so
far because, believe me, they can be most unjust in their
actions toward ordinary people like you and I.

Of course that might be hard for you to see, but even you
must begin to wonder when returning Korean ex-prisoners
of war are put in jail for speaking truth. Or else they are put
out of the way in "mental hospitals." Well, Sis, I'm hoping
very much that I will be able to see you but you will have to
realize that it will only be possible by you coming to see me
for my decision to remain here is stronger than ever, and was
made of my own free will. My reasons, when you fully understand them, you may want to stay here yourself. . . .

If you come to see me, don't come thinking I'm some hor-
rible creature with horns and everything. . . . For I am still
your brother, hardly changed at all except that I am now a
bit more clearsighted. . . . Keep your ears open and when
you go back home think everything over carefully and you
may then be a wiser woman. . . .

Your loving brother, Bud,
Aaron P. Wilson

No passport was forthcoming, but William L. Randall of
nearby Olla, then with the 374th Troop Carriers in Tokyo,
flew over to Panmunjom to try to argue him out of it. He
never got a chance and only saw Aaron from a distance.

When Batchelor came out, he revealed that both Aaron's
letter and another sent by Tenneson to his mother had been
a joint composition of the group.

When the deadline came and went and Aaron was lost behind the Iron Curtain, Mrs. Wilson still insisted that if he could have been separated from the others he would have come home.

"I still say he'd come home if he could get away. My boy is scared to death. He's scared to come home. It's more than I can bear."

Pvt. Samuel David Hawkins

of Oklahoma City, Okla.

born August 11, 1933

enlisted September 21, 1949

2nd Division

captured November 30, 1950

Protestant

3rd year high school

low-average I.Q.

The Army Reported:

According to returned prisoners of war, Hawkins voluntarily collaborated with the Communists, informed *on his fellow prisoners, attended voluntary classes conducted by the Chinese and tried to persuade other prisoners to accept Communism. Among other rewards, Hawkins was appointed mail clerk by the Chinese.*

To his mother, David Hawkins was "a baby in a man's shoes." To his fellow prisoners of war in a Korean prison camp, he was "a character, a fresh kid." To his teachers in Oklahoma City, he was a dreamer "who wanted to get through the day with the least disturbance; who took life as it came and didn't put up much fight."

Samuel David Hawkins was only sixteen when he enlisted in the army, with his mother's signature and records to prove he was seventeen. He was really seventeen when he was captured by the Chinese Reds in the disorganized 2nd Division retreat of late November, 1950. He was twenty when he was persuaded to stay back with the rest of the twenty-one American prisoners of war who refused repatriation.

His mother, Mrs. Carley Sallee Jones, a twice-divorced Holiness sect preacher, signed for her only child's enlistment in 1949 because "I didn't want him running loose in the streets; there wasn't a war on then." She couldn't know that he would never run loose anywhere, ever again.

"I'm sure I was too strict with him," Mrs. Jones said when she first heard the news that her son was among those who would not return. "I raised him as a little fellow, not to engage in worldly things, I guess you'd just have to say. Outside of church and Boy Scouts, he just didn't have any other activities. Oh, he read comic books—you couldn't keep him from it—and when he got old enough to make a choice I let him go to the movies, although it wasn't in my faith. But that was about all."

Her last letter from David was sent on May 11, 1953, and he "didn't even mention that he wanted to stay behind; all of his letters asked us to pray for him that he would come home soon."

David's father, Clayton O. Hawkins, an oil field worker, died in a fire in Tuskahoma, Okla., while his son was in prison camp. The Hawkinses had been divorced when David was a youngster, but the boy had kept some contact with his father, visiting him at his rooming house when he was in Oklahoma City—"but usually only when he wanted money," according to the landlord there.

His mother's second marriage didn't last much longer than her first. David never had a settled home. His mother moved from rooming house to rooming house, from one section of Oklahoma City to another. One year he went to three different schools.

Sometimes the boy stayed with his grandmother, Mrs. Herbert E. Slaughter, and it was her name that was put down on his enlistment papers for notification. Mrs. Slaughter thought her daughter had been pretty hard on David. She was resentful over what happened to him and blamed it on the democratic administration.

"What were we fighting for over there anyway?" she asked. "They gave our boys tanks without nuts and bolts, things that wouldn't work. They didn't try to win the war."

Because he moved around so much and because his life was so hemmed in with maternal restraints, David never had a chance to make any close friends in Oklahoma City. One summer he went out to California to visit an aunt and was so happy there with his cousins that he begged to stay—and did for two years.

—112

Since his uncle is an army officer, the family refuses to reveal his name, evidently from some of the same feelings that David himself expressed to fellow prisoners of war in camp when he made his decision to stay—although he twisted the facts a bit.

"Sure I'm staying," he told a hut mate. "But I don't know what they'll do to my old man. He's a major in the German occupation army."

At school, his teachers had liked David—one remembered every seat he had sat in—though some of them thought him unresponsive, even to kind treatment, and said he was not a happy boy. His I.Q. was 96, a little below average (which is 100), but he didn't do as well in school as he could have because of "lack of effort."

He got along well both with teachers and classmates. He was not a troublemaker, but he had no close friends, no buddy, no girl, no interest in sports or extracurricular activities.

One teacher said he had talked to her about his doubts of his mother's religious beliefs and felt that he had been pressured into church activities. His grandmother was inclined to agree and thought he went to church because he was forced to go.

David was absent from school a good deal all through the years, but after he returned from California to start his third year in high school he was particularly restless and often stayed away from class. Finally he quit going altogether and it was then that his mother signed for his enlistment "to keep him off the streets."

Mrs. Jones was hard to track down to the modest frame rooming house where she lives in the northwest section of Oklahoma City. With reporters she had been alternately talkative and belligerently silent. When I finally found her home, she stood behind a door at the top of the stairs and declared she had nothing to say except that she was writing the story of her son's life herself.

On January 28, 1954, the day he left for China, she had written an article about him for the Oklahoma City *Times,* after first refusing to look at wire photos of the group.

"I feel like heading a one-woman army and going after those kids myself," her story started.

"If you ask me who has disgraced themselves, it is we, who have sat back in apparent helplessness and let those Red devils carry off twenty-one of our American boys, and for propaganda purposes of our own say, 'Good riddance to bad rubbish.'

"One of those boys happens to be mine and I'm not going to let the Communists push me around while I sit idly by and say and do nothing. For, I'm serving a living God.

"It reminds me of a like story in I Samuel 17, where the giant Goliath defied the army of the living God and little David with the shepherd's sling and five stones met the challenge with, 'Who is the uncircumcised Philistine that he should defy the army of the living God?' "

Mrs. Jones told of how her son had written home for pictures of late model cars and of the fact that he, like most of the rest, had $5,000 waiting for him, as a basis for her belief that his refusal to come home could not be "voluntary."

She spoke of "the great mistake" she made in "not teaching him more self-reliance instead of fighting his battles for him and shielding him from the realities of life so closely that he was unable physically, mentally and spiritually to cope with the situation he faced in prison.

"The anguish he must have suffered in soul and body, as all boys did, but some with more fortitude than these twenty-one."

—114

When she signed for his enlistment in the army she said she "did not take into consideration that the reason for having an army is in the event of war." David didn't even know what he was fighting for, Mrs. Jones pointed out, adding, "For that matter does anyone realize what the Korean war was all about?

"I shudder when I think of the time David wakes up to what Communism really is and that they deny the Lord Jesus Christ in Whom he has believed all his life."

In conclusion she wrote, "Let him who is without sin cast the first stone at these boys. Judge not, lest ye be judged."

No longer a stripling, but filled out and strikingly handsome, the day Samuel David Hawkins left for China he scoffed at a suggestion from a correspondent that some of the group had been "bought."

"Don't the people realize that each of us had about $5,000 in back pay which he could have collected if he went back?"

Hawkins also protested what he called the "prosecution and persecution of Dickenson" who had left the group, citing courtmartial charges which were then being prepared against him.

His mother said at that time that she believed that without divine help, her son would stay with the Communists.

"But with God's help there is no Iron Curtain," she added. "If their god is stronger than my God, they can keep him. Under God's will everything works for the best. But if I could see David now, I'd try to tell him he'd be better off in prison here in this country than he would be with freedom, over there."

Pfc. William C. White

of Plumerville, Ark.

born May 9, 1930

enlisted March 17, 1948

2nd Division

captured November 30, 1950

Negro, Protestant

4th year high school

average I.Q.

The Army Reported:

> *According to returned prisoners of war, White informed on his fellow prisoners, willingly accepted Communist ideology, and tried to influence other prisoners to accept Communism. Among his rewards was the position of mailman.*

THE FEW THAT REMEMBER HIM are puzzled—but not many remember him. His mother and his teachers are "crushed"; it wasn't like him.

For the first time in his life, William C. White of Plumerville, Ark., population 550, is a member of a group. This might be cause for rejoicing except that the group happens to be the twenty-one American prisoners of war who turned their backs on their country and headed for China with their Red captors.

"Kind of indifferent," a boy who grew up with him, called him. "During recess he'd go off and sit by himself. Boy came near him, he'd just move farther off. Never made no fuss about it. Just wanted to be by himself."

"A good worker," said a white farmer, who hired him summers to work his cotton and corn. "Not one of those rowdy niggers. You couldn't find a nicer boy."

"He was a likable youngster," said one of his teachers, "never in trouble with anyone, in or out of school."

Folks in Plumerville are even more puzzled by the statement he made just before he left for China than by his decision to stay with the Reds. He said then:

"I have been in prison for three years, and for the first time in my life, I have seen complete equality for men of all races and colors who worked together and played together. When I see things like this I am reminded of what happened to me in my own country where as children, I and other Negro boys were whipped by policemen because we didn't take off our hats to them."

There aren't any policemen in Plumerville. No one remembers William being whipped by anyone for anything. His mother, Mrs. Mattie Lee Gorman, said she didn't know what he was talking about.

"I never heard of him being whipped by a policeman. He's just saying what he's been made to say, that's all."

His mother and his stepfather, Walter Gorman, are well thought of in Plumerville, a hamlet some fifty miles from Little Rock, Arkansas' capital. They pay their bills regularly and aren't "in" to the local store.

Gorman works as a trackwalker for the railroad, an off again, on again job, and Mrs. Gorman supplements his income by working in a rural garment factory in Morrilton, the next town down the pike.

Plumerville is a farm village set in the midst of rich bottomland that produces a good crop of cotton and corn and soy beans. There are not many trees and the sun shines down relentlessly. The back roads are dusty on the rises and pools of water in the dips. The Negro community where the Gormans live lies along a dirt road on a ridge back of the main road. Just before the road reaches the Gorman home, it dips and the ford looked too much for my rented car, so I got out and walked. No one was home in the neat white painted cottage and neighbors directed me to the garment factory where Mrs. Gorman works.

I talked to her during her lunch hour at the factory, where she is one of a long row of women at machines, stitching the seams of men's work slacks. Mrs. Gorman is strong and young-looking, usually good-natured and serene, but now she was worried and puzzled.

—120

"I don't understand it at all," she told me. "He never wrote me about wanting to stay over there. Never wrote about anything like that. He wrote some funny letters but always he talked about coming home."

Mrs. Gorman divorced William's father before the boy was a year old and remarried soon afterward.

"My mother raised him until he was five," Mrs. Gorman told me. "But she lived down the road a piece and I saw him every day. After that he lived some with her and some with us."

His grandmother is dead now, she added. He got along well with his two younger half brothers and his half sister, she thought—"the girl was my favorite." He was a good boy who liked to go to school and did pretty well in school. His nickname was "W. C." and he didn't have any special friends that she could remember.

He wanted to study medicine and be a doctor, his mother remembered, but he left high school with a semester to go before graduation to enlist in the army in March of 1948.

"He went up to Kansas City to stay with his aunt and went to high school there for a term," Mrs. Gorman said. "He enlisted up there. I guess he went in because he thought he could study medicine under the G.I.

"He didn't write any of those letters about Communism," Mrs. Gorman said. "I don't know what this is all about. I've been wondering what is this Communism. And I've been wondering if he don't want to come home, why he can't write me and tell me so right out."

William went to a four-room segregated Negro school on the outskirts of Plumerville, a school made from native stone as a PWA project. The teachers who were there when he was, and the young principal who had been a classmate of his, admit that they never really knew the boy. At high school he is not even remembered.

At the combination filling station and general store near the Gorman home, the owners had nothing but praise for the Gormans and for William White.

"They've been trading here for more than eight years and they never buy what they can't afford and they always pay their bills. William was a pretty nice and intelligent boy, like his mother and stepfather. He loved to hunt and fish but he never got in any trouble."

That is, not until he enlisted in the army in March of 1948. He went into Korea with the 2nd Division and fought through the early phases of the war, the early defeats, the illusory victory and then the great retreat when the Chinese hordes were thrown into battle. He was captured on December 1, 1950, and had been a prisoner for more than three years when he went off to China with the rest of the twenty-one.

He didn't mix in prison any better than he had at home, returned prisoners of war said. But there were always prison walls to keep him from moving further away when he wanted to be alone.

And the Chinese Communists knew how to turn to their own uses his sense of being an outsider even in his own home where everyone carried a different name than he did and where he hadn't grown up anyway.

Cpl. Harold H. Webb

of Jacksonville, Fla.

born September 12, 1931

enlisted August 2, 1949

captured December 1, 1950

Protestant

9th grade

low-average I.Q.

The Army Reported:

According to returned prisoners of war, Webb informed *on fellow prisoners, wrote propaganda articles, made Communist propaganda posters, circulated petitions, made propaganda broadcast recordings, and became a member of the "Kremlin Club." His rewards included elevation to the post of camp librarian.*

Eight years ago a skinny, undernourished kid named Harold Webb was attending eighth grade classes at the Westgate Junior High School in a suburb of West Palm Beach—attending them but little more. He didn't like school. He came only to play football, for which he had a passion so strong that he braved beatings with a window sash, beatings that left raw open welts across his back, to continue playing.

"He was skinny but he was strong and tough as a piece of whiplash," a teacher who knew him in those days and saw the welts on his back, told me. "He made up his mind he was going to play football and he did. When I saw his name in the paper as one of the twenty-one who were going to stay over there I tried to figure out in my mind why that boy would do it. He was a good boy. But he didn't have anything to come home for. Anything they offered him would be better than what he had."

Six years ago Harold Webb enlisted in the army and a year or so later he was captured in the winter rout. In January of 1954, still skinny and undernourished, he told reporters at Panmunjom before he left for China that he wanted his father and his sister to know that he was very happy.

"I hope they will understand," he said. "If they don't now, I hope they will in the future."

His father has disappeared. His sister Katherine, who at

twenty-two is happily married, with three children including twins, doesn't understand. She and her husband, a veteran of World War II who also saw peacetime service in Korea, had set aside a room in their attractive West Palm Beach home for her brother.

A gentle, pretty girl who didn't want to talk about her brother, she couldn't quite bring herself to turn me away. She was seeking some clue in her own mind and asked for details of the lives of the others of the twenty-one.

When I told her about Richard Corden who had been beaten by his father with the buckle end of a belt, she began to cry softly. She wiped her tears away and sat up straighter. She seemed to come to some decision.

"My brother went to school over there in Westgate," she said. "He lived with my father for a time after my mother and grandmother died."

I knew she expected me to find the story she could not bring herself to tell, the story of the boy who went to school with welts on his back.

Harold was born in Jacksonville, Fla., in 1931. Both his parents were native Floridians. Mrs. Webb had been one of the three pretty Hunter girls, brought up by a stepmother who continued to care for them as her own after their father died.

After the girls were grown, the second Mrs. Hunter married Irving Carpenter and the two were acting as caretakers for the S. S. Simmons estate, Pop-o-Lee, at Mandarin, eighteen miles out of Jacksonville, when Mrs. Webb brought her two children there to live. She turned to her stepmother when her marriage broke up.

The beautiful broad lawns of the estate stretch down to the St. Johns River and Harold and Katherine played on the banks and roamed through the semitropical glades. They

—126

went to school at nearby Loretto. These were halcyon days. But they were not to last. Mrs. Webb had never been well, but her death was a sudden shock. Her stepmother survived her for only a few months. The children were separated, Katherine going to an aunt in West Palm Beach and Harold to his father who was working off and on as a carpenter in Westgate.

Harold's school record had been poor at Loretto and it was worse in Westgate. He had failed two subjects in the ninth grade and had been absent ten days when he dropped out of school in 1947 not long before he was sixteen. He went on his own then, getting a job first with a Venetian blind company in West Palm Beach and then with a sheet metal company in Miami. In the spring of 1949 he came up to Fort Pierce, Fla., and stayed with an aunt, Mrs. Evelyn Klipstein. He worked part time for a sign company, tried to enlist in the navy and failing that, enlisted in the army in August, a month before his eighteenth birthday.

He was in the ill-fated 2nd Division and was made a prisoner on December 1, 1950, when the Chinese infiltrated a roadblock guarding the general withdrawal of his regiment. Returned prisoners of war who knew him in camp remember him as a boy who stayed to himself, "a strange one," an early progressive but not a particularly strong one.

His letters home were fairly cheerful and had little propaganda in them. He wrote his aunt in December of 1952, after he had been a prisoner for two years, that he was "still the same old guy that left home three years ago; there's only one change and that is that I'm not a kid any more. I'm a man now with a few thousand miles under my feet."

He assured his aunt that he was "still not a drinking man" and that there was nothing to worry about, "just keep your fingers crossed and I'll be home soon."

He spoke of a big fishing trip he would take with his uncle when he got home and then wrote:

Well, I guess I'd better close for now for I'm running out of space to write. Say, before I close, how about sending me some pictures of the family. Say, tell Mary Ann (a neighborhood girl) to send me some pictures too that is if she doesn't mind.

Say, I'm sorry I won't be able to spend this Xmas with you but maybe I'll be there for the one next year. I wish you all a very Merry Christmas and a Happy New Year.

The next Christmas he was in the neutral compound in Panmunjom. His sister was not prepared for the shock of finding out that he wouldn't return. She felt sure he was being kept against his will. Her husband laid daring plans for a blood and thunder forced rescue.

"If I just could have gotten over there," he said, "I know that section backward and forward and you can do anything in Korea with a little money. I'd have gotten him out of that camp and back home."

"We wanted him to live with us," Katherine added. "Why, he's never seen the children. He was such a cute little boy himself, with his slanted black eyes and dark hair. We taught him to call himself 'Little Jap.'"

As he prepared to leave for the interior of China, Webb made the usual statement:

"Here I can speak freely for world peace. I can't do that in America as Dickenson has already found out (he had just been held for courtmartial) and as Batchelor will find out. They didn't try Dickenson until after it was all over because they thought they could fool us and get others of us to come back."

Harold H. Webb

His sister received a New Year's message from him sent by radio and mail, but otherwise there has been no word from him since he made his decision not to return to his home and country.

Pfc. Clarence Adams

of Memphis, Tenn.

born January 4, 1929

enlisted 1947

24th Division

captured December 1, 1950

Negro, Protestant

3rd year high school

average I.Q.

The Army Reported:

According to returned prisoners of war, Adams voluntarily collaborated with his captors and used his efforts and influence to urge fellow prisoners to accept Communism. He circulated petitions prepared by the Communists to further their war aims and he urged other prisoners to sign them. He attended special classes in political economy. He was an informant *to the Chinese on activities of loyal Americans held prisoner. As a reward for his efforts he was selected by the Chinese to be a librarian.*

"I<small>F</small> I <small>DON'T GET BACK</small>, you'll know I've done my best," Clarence (Skippy) Adams wrote to his mother from the front lines in Korea in the fall of 1950, just about the time he would have been mustered out from his three-year enlistment if there hadn't been a war on.

Skippy didn't get back. Did he do his best? No one who knew the quiet, lonely, delicate boy when he was growing up in Memphis, Tenn., doubts but that he did—even though the reason he didn't get back was because he was one of the twenty-one who refused repatriation.

They don't pretend to understand how Skippy got to the point of no return. They just go by what they knew of him at school, at work and at play, a kid who tried to the limits of his capacities, who never got in trouble in his life, who always wanted to do his best—to do better than his best.

Like the two other Negro prisoners of war who didn't come back, Clarence made a bitter statement at Panmunjom about "race prejudice and segregation."

However much he might have felt such bitterness in his childhood, it had never been obvious to those who knew him best.

"Those words were not Skippy's," said one of his teachers. "He didn't leave Memphis with any of those feelings. The average colored boy faces up to the segregation and accepts it and goes on about his business."

His mother, Mrs. Gladys Peoples, too, discounted the effects of race prejudice. "Skippy encountered less of it than the average colored boy," she told me. "He grew up in a white neighborhood and played with white boys as a child."

His high school teachers did not agree. They felt that the race situation could not but affect Clarence or any other Negro.

Clarence's childhood home was a tenant house on the old "Coward Place," a pre-Civil War mansion which has been engulfed by the city. His mother remarried when he was not yet two years old and although his stepfather "couldn't have been nicer to him," the boy was conscious that he was an outsider in the family. He was the only one with the Adams name.

Since his was the only Negro family in the area, there were none but white boys with whom he could play. He did not go to school with them, but to the nearest segregated Negro school.

As a result he had no close pal, no friend that he carried on with from home to school or school to home.

"He was a wonderful kid," a former neighbor reminisced sadly. "Everybody liked him. He was amenable as can be, never any trouble to anyone."

His mother thought he had always been a good boy with a strong conscience. He helped around the house, did dishes and straightened up his own room and when he was old enough, worked after school as a dishwasher in local hospitals.

"When he was little, if I scolded him he would say, 'I did it, Toosie, but I'm going to do better.' When he did do anything wrong, he cried so hard while you were cutting the switch that you didn't hardly use it on him."

He never got into fights with other boys, nor was he

picked on. As a child his favorite occupation was to play Tarzan and swing from limb to limb of the big trees in the yard of the Coward Place but as he grew older he took an interest in boxing.

School was no problem at first but times came when he begged for a "day off," although he never played hooky "without permission."

"He was a sweet boy," his fourth grade teacher said, "the kind of child you fell for at first sight. But it was hard to draw him out. He was shy and quiet, easily influenced, not at all aggressive and nearly always alone."

When he was ten, Clarence was seriously ill with high blood pressure and an edema from which he recovered slowly. His teachers thought that he never had really good health from then on.

His fifth grade teacher felt he was overshadowed by his four brilliant young half-sisters—he was the only boy.

"One of them caught up to him in school," she told me. "And they were all outgoing and well adjusted and unusually bright. Clarence had to work hard for every grade he got and he did work hard. Too hard. He was overanxious to get his lesson right and was on the verge of tears when he didn't."

Other teachers thought he was "too quiet, too meek," that it was hard to get him to "express an opinion on anything." At the Booker T. Washington High School, which his mother had also attended, it was the same at first. But he grew restless and bored with school; his mother worried over his attitude and had many conferences with school officials.

"He thought maybe if he got away from school and went into the army he would go back and do better when he came out," Mrs. Peoples told me. "That's why I agreed to his enlistment."

Clarence enlisted in September of 1947. Three years later when his enlistment would have been up he was in the fighting lines in Korea with the 24th Division, the first United States forces to be sent in against the North Koreans. He went through the early defeats, the "victory march" to the Yalu and the first brushes against the Chinese in October. Capture came during the disastrous retreat when the Chinese put their full forces into the field right after Thanksgiving. Clarence was reported missing on December 1.

It was awhile before Mrs. Peoples heard from her son, but soon afterward she was not only hearing from him but from strangers all over the world and being bombarded with pamphlets and copies of Communist newspapers.

Mrs. Monica Felton, former Labor member of the British Parliament, was allowed by the Chinese to visit the prison camps during the long-drawn-out peace conferences and she wrote that Clarence, whom she called "the son of an oppressed mother in Memphis," was "taking part in the peace movement and discussions."

Still Mrs. Peoples was not prepared for the news that her son was not coming home.

Clarence had taken an active part in the affairs of his church, the Metropolitan Baptist, and was a church member. He attended Sunday School regularly and in his teens joined the Men's Bible Class. From prison camp he wrote a letter to the pastor, the Reverend S. A. Queen, asking for prayers for peace; it was read to the congregation.

But neighbors and members of the congregation felt that the whole family had been perhaps a little aloof from their church and from other community groups. There were some who thought their attitude snobbish.

The Peoples family now live in a neat little house of their

own in a new Negro development on the outskirts of Memphis. Mrs. Peoples works as a laundry checker and evenings baby sits with one of her daughter's children.

Clarence's picture in uniform is on top of the piano in the nicely furnished living room. It is the only home I visited where there was a piano. Mrs. Peoples is small and trim, well dressed and well spoken.

She is not impressed by the barrage of Red propaganda she was still receiving long after her son went behind the Iron Curtain, from as far away as Czechoslovakia, nor by the letters she got from returned prisoners of war who swallowed the Communist line. Nor does she believe that her son is a Communist.

"They must have doped them or used hypnosis," she said, "then got them to do something they wouldn't have done otherwise. Then they would be afraid to come back, for fear of punishment. They never let them hear any of the good side of the news but just what they wanted them to hear. I wrote him and tried to keep him abreast of what was really happening but they didn't let him get but two of my letters."

All of her son's letters spoke of what he wanted to do "when he got home," she said, "and then they stopped coming.

"His heart wasn't in it, wasn't in staying over there," she said. "He couldn't write me and tell me he wasn't coming home."

Mrs. Peoples and one of her daughters journeyed to Chicago to make a recording to send to Clarence but, like the others, it was never heard by him.

Since May of 1953 she has heard directly from him once, a message dated December 31 and received January 20, 1954, saying:

Wish family a bright future in the coming year. In best health.

Love,

Skippy.

Peiping Radio has since quoted him as saying he was "confident that my future in China will be as bright as my new suit," when he and the other twenty-one went into civilian clothes.

A returned prisoner of war, himself a progressive, who knew him in Camp V, the camp for progressives, expressed his surprise that Clarence had stayed behind.

"He was not a strong progressive," his fellow prisoner said. "You wouldn't have thought he would even have thought about staying. He was usually a calm and quiet boy, but sometimes could be quick and changeable. He jumped on me one day when we were digging an air raid trench. I suggested that we dig deeper. He said if he felt like that—that our own men would bomb us—he wouldn't go back to the States."

Other Negroes with whom I talked felt they were saved by two things. One was that plenty of them had been "gone over" by Communists at home before they enlisted and had reached the point of disillusionment. Those that knew "wised up the rest of us." The other was the high-pressure tactics that backfired. "They told us there wasn't any segregation in Communist countries and then they segregated us, put the Negroes all together in Camp V."

Because Clarence held aloof from his fellows, these factors did not count so much with him. Late in February of 1954, Peiping Radio quoted him from behind the Iron Curtain as saying "with strong emotion" as he arrived in Manchuria, that he had "racial equality" for the first time in his life. There has been no word of him since then.

Pfc. Arlie H. Pate

of East Carondelet, Ill.

born November 3, 1931

enlisted January 12, 1949

7th Division

captured December 2, 1950

Baptist

9th grade

average I.Q.

The Army Reported:

According to returned prisoners of war, Pate's willingness to cooperate with the Communists resulted in his appointment to the staff of the camp newspaper. He circulated petitions, wrote articles for the Communist publication Toward Truth and Peace, *made recordings for propaganda purposes and informed on prisoners who attempted to escape or who refused to accept Communism. His rewards included better food and clothing, better medical care and a large degree of freedom.*

"I<small>F I RAISED MY VOICE</small> it was like hitting him with a whip."
Hersel Lillis, manager of the Broadhead Motor Company
in East St. Louis, Ill., was talking of Arlie Pate, who grew up
in the levee country of southern Illinois.

"Arlie walked in one day when he was sixteen and asked
for a job," Lillis, a big, bluff, friendly man told me. "He
looked like he needed work and we needed a boy so we took
him on. He was a good worker. There was nobody around
here who didn't like him. But I soon found out that when I
went looking for him I would have to be careful or I would
scare him."

Arlie's job was with the parts department. He drove a
truck on short errands, picking up parts. He was a little
"slow" and "we would have to write down each of the stops
we wanted him to make," his immediate superiors recalled.
But he "didn't try to make time on the job like a lot of
others." He earned $25 a week and gave half of it to his
mother.

"Arlie was a big, good-looking boy who was bound to fill
out and get bigger," Lillis told me. "When he enlisted he
came down to see us and show off his uniform. He was real
proud of it. He hadn't seen much in his life but poverty and
hard times. He enlisted because he wanted to see the world,
he said, but all he saw was the Korean battlefields and a
prison stockade. He was the last kid in the world you'd pick

for a Communist—and yet I can see that he would probably believe anything they told him."

In East Carondelet, Arlie's sister Goldie, now Mrs. Cecil Sloan, with three attractive young children of her own, lives across the way from the makeshift house where she and Arlie grew up. She agreed that life had been kind of bleak when she and Arlie were youngsters.

"Our clothes were ragged and we were on relief and the other kids picked on us a lot," she told me as she spooned cereal into the baby, Arlene. "For myself, I didn't mind too much. I got along all right. But Arlie minded. He didn't fight back; he took it to heart. Every day he came straight home from school to get away from it."

For Arlie, it was the last straw when a new pair of slacks he had worked hard to buy were stolen from his locker at high school while he was in gym class, two hard-earned dollars taken from the pockets and the slacks stuffed down the drain.

"He got the slacks back," Mrs. Sloan said, "but they couldn't be made fit to wear. And he never got the $2.00. That was when he quit school. I tried my best to talk him out of it, but I couldn't. Later he was sorry and that was one reason he went in the army. He wasn't a happy kid. My father wasn't well and he didn't get along with him."

On their new farm, nine miles down dirt roads from Carbondale, Ill., Arlie's parents, Mr. and Mrs. Daniel Howard Pate, told me how they had never expected Arlie would go into battle when they signed for his enlistment at seventeen, in 1949.

It was late in the afternoon when I set out to find the Pate place. It had rained for three days and the back roads were slippery ruts. I had the usual country directions. "Turn left, then go past the church and turn right at the next fork, then left, then cross a creek," and so on. As the miles slid by I began to feel lost but I passed a car at the side of the road and asked if this was the way to the Pate farm.

"It sure is the way but I don't know if you can make it," was the answer.

There were several times when I was sure he was right, but I got through to the last hill and there I began slipping back two feet for every one I could advance. On the top of the hill a boy sat on a horse.

"Go back," he shouted, "go back to the bottom of the hill."

I obeyed and he galloped down and showed me where I could turn.

"Where you trying to go?" he asked.

"I'm looking for the Pate place," I said.

"I'm Donald," he said. "It's right up here," he pointed.

He led the way and I followed through the fields.

On the way up to the comfortable seven-room farmhouse, I found out that my guide was Donald Pate, age fourteen, and that he had a twin named Ronald. When I left, as darkness was settling down over the empty lonely landscape, Donald piloted me back to my car, and sheer luck got me to the highway.

Arlie has never seen the farm, and though it was his oft-repeated ambition to have a family farm, he didn't even know it had been achieved when he made his "decision" to stay with the Chinese Reds.

Arlie's parents can't account for what happened to their son. The statements he made in televised interviews and to reporters before he left for the interior of China just don't make sense to them.

"I thought I understood Arlie," said his mother, small, plump and very tired, as she sat in the dimly lit living room, seven of her nine living children around her. "Anybody could understand him.

"He didn't have any close friends," she added, "and played mostly with his sister. He wasn't allowed to fight and he didn't. He minded mighty good and if he couldn't have what he wanted he accepted it, gave up."

His father said that Arlie didn't like to do things by himself, "he liked to work with the other fellow."

Growing up he played mostly with his brothers and sisters, but Goldie was always his favorite. He helped around the house and shared whatever he had and was a "good boy who went to Sunday School and church." He never got into trouble. Neither politics nor Communism was ever discussed at home and when he left for Korea, his folks felt, he knew nothing about either.

Arlie's family have lived in southern Illinois, in the coal mining area chiefly not far from the new farm, for four generations. His grandfather and namesake, Arlie Howard Pate, was killed in an accident at Blair's mine near Murphysboro. His great grandfather, Anthony Pate, founded Pate's Chapel. On his mother's side his great grandfather, John Kelley, was a Baptist minister, reputed able "to put the fear of God in any man." From prison camp Arlie wrote that when he got back home he'd like "to do the same thing grandfather did."

Arlie was born in an old company house in a rundown mine district near Herrin, notorious for disasters and labor-management troubles in the late Twenties. His father worked the mines there until he was laid off because of his epilepsy.

Before Arlie was school age, the family moved to East Carondelet. This is river bottom country, levee country, where the Mississippi floods every few years despite the levee.

When that happens the families are evacuated to the high school at nearby Dupo—the school Arlie attended a short time—and the Red Cross sets up cots in the school and feeds and cares for the refugees. Sometimes the Red Cross has a hard time getting them to go back to their mud-encrusted homes when the floodwaters go down, because life has been so much easier and pleasanter.

Arlie is remembered in grammar school as "well-mannered," a boy who was never a discipline problem, docile, a follower with no push. Of average I.Q., he didn't do well in school at first, but by sixth grade was closer to the class average. He was silent and melancholy, a boy who was never chosen by his classmates for anything, who didn't make friends or have a girl, despite his good looks.

All during his school days his family was on relief—"aid for dependent children." Teachers felt that all the children were timid and felt inferior because of their hand-me-down clothes.

Arlie's father built a house out of savings from the relief payments and old lumber they picked up, which led to the first stroke of good luck the family ever had. He was able to trade the house for the sixty-two-acre farm they now have—but this was after Arlie was in prison camp.

When Arlie quit high school he first went to stay with his grandmother on her farm not far from where his family is now living. He did odd jobs and was happy there. Neighbors remember him as a "likely" boy who didn't "drink, smoke or swear." He left the farm reluctantly and went to East St. Louis to get his job with the Broadhead Motor Company because he knew how much his family needed his help.

After he enlisted he came home on leave once in the spring of 1950 and then was shipped to Tokyo. He sent home pictures of himself cheek to cheek with a Japanese girl, the first girl he had ever had. Then came June 25, 1950. Arlie went into the line with the 7th Division, after the Inchon landings in September. He was reported missing December 2 as his division was fighting its way to a beachhead on the coast to be taken out by ship, as it had been landed.

In his letters home he mentioned the good treatment he was getting—"We're treated so wonderfully over here"—and the good meals, including pork and fish as well as maize and rice. Some of the letters didn't sound like him, his family said. But he also wrote about his longing to come back and work on a farm and of how he prayed that he would get back. In one single letter he referred seven times to coming home.

He wrote his mother that he would be released "as soon as a peace treaty is signed and a democratic line established at the 38th parallel." But he also said:

"Tell Viola (his sister) to write and tell me how she is getting along and if she doesn't I will take care of her when I get home. Tell Daniel I was sorry I was not able to be at their wedding and tell him that when I get home I will make it up to him."

Still, when he was "tapped" to be one of the group that would refuse repatriation, there were plenty of angles for the Chinese to twist against him.

When he was interviewed at Panmunjom just before he disappeared behind the Iron Curtain, Arlie said:

"It is impossible to fight for peace in the United States. Anyone who tries to fight for peace will be prosecuted and even put to death. The Rosenbergs spoke out for peace and look what the United States government did to them."

"The Rosenbergs were convicted on a charge of treason as atomic spies," a correspondent put in, "and executed upon

—146

conviction. But you say they were executed because they spoke out for peace."

"The treason was a trumped-up charge," Arlie declared. "The only thing they were guilty of was speaking out for peace. Now they are trying to try ex-President Truman on House Un-American Committee charges."

Arlie got that last from the same source as his information about the Rosenbergs. Like most, if not all, of the rest his ignorance of politics and especially of Communism had been complete.

East Carondelet folks who saw him on television said he talked and acted like a complete stranger—"not the same boy that left here."

And his sister Goldie said wistfully, "People were kinder to Arlie when this happened."

Cpl. Howard Gayle Adams

of Corsicana, Tex.

born May 29, 1925

Bronze Star for Heroism

World War II

re-enlisted August 31, 1948

24th Division

captured January 1, 1951

Baptist

3½ years college

average I.Q.

The Army Reported:

According to returned prisoners of war, Adams quickly became a willing follower of the Communist ideology and attempted to influence other prisoners to accept Communism. He collaborated with his captors by making recordings for broadcast, writing propaganda articles for camp newspapers, circulating petitions and urging fellow prisoners to sign them, and kept Communist authorities informed of activities of other prisoners. As a part of the rewards tendered him, Adams was appointed by the Chinese to serve on a mess committee.

I<small>N</small> 1945, Howard Gayle Adams of Corsicana, Tex., was given the Bronze Star for his courage in combat in the Asiatic-Pacific theater.

In 1954, he was given a dishonorable discharge for his refusal to accept repatriation as one of the twenty-one American prisoners of war who stayed with their Red captors.

Gayle, as he was known in his home town, was a serious-minded youth who tried hard to live up to his own high standards. It is revealing that his citation for the Bronze Star reads, "For exemplary conduct on the field of battle." His conduct had always been exemplary.

"I would have been happier if he had chucked an eraser now and then," one of his teachers said. "When boys are boys, you are reassured."

That Gayle had wanted to chuck an eraser on occasion, even if he never did, was revealed in a letter he wrote to his teacher from prison camp:

"When I first took English, I didn't like it, or you either, but I have come to know how important what you tried to teach me is."

Gayle is the oldest of three boys. His father, J. H. Adams, was an oil field worker during the years the boys were growing up and he was seldom at home. At present he is living in Houston while Mrs. Adams still lives in Corsicana, working at a nursing home.

Raising her three boys was a struggle for Mrs. Adams, who has earned the respect and affection of all who know her in Corsicana.

"I don't know how she managed on what she could get together," a friend told me. "It was a meager existence. But she managed. She kept the boys in school and she kept them going to Sunday School and she got them every place on time. She took an active interest in PTA work even when she was living on the edge of a wealthy section of town and all the other women had fine clothes and cars. Her whole life was dedicated to her boys. She is a wonderful woman."

Corsicana is one of the wealthier Texas towns with a two-fold oil boom background. Back in 1897 the first shallow fields were found. Again in 1920 the town boomed when deep fields were discovered. They are still pumping oil around Corsicana but the town's wealth is based also on the cotton harvested from the nearby "black land belt" and from stock raising. There is a sharp cleavage between the rich and the poor, who are mostly tenant farmers and laborers who wander away when the work falls off.

Life on the tenant farms, such as the one Gayle Adams' family rented during part of his boyhood, can be bleak and lonely. I spent most of a day on one waiting in vain for a former fellow prisoner of Gayle's to return home. His young wife, who had cleaned and polished the sparsely furnished, rugless, four-room tenant house to a high brilliance, was glad of company. Her nearest neighbor was more than two miles away down rutted, unshaded roads and her husband had the car.

"I expected him home for dinner," she told me when I first came, but as the day waned she admitted they had quarreled and she didn't know when he'd be home. We started out in search of him then, missing him by an hour or so every place we trailed him. I brought her back to her neighbor's home, gayer now because of the outing. I still don't know if or when her husband came back. They had no phone.

Tracing Mrs. Adams, who had moved recently, was just as difficult. The end of the trail, there, was at a hospital where she was a patient with pneumonia. She wasn't talking about her son to anyone any more—not since the last days of grace had come and gone for Gayle.

When Gayle was growing up the family moved often and the boys went to several different schools in Corsicana and the surrounding area. For awhile they lived on a farm near a village called Blooming Grove, a few miles out of town. It was described as "the poorest piece of land in a section where the land generally is as poor as you can find."

It was at that time that Gayle's father, on one of his rare visits home, bought a pedigreed Jersey bull. The boys had to lead the bull up and down the highway to get enough grass to keep it alive. It didn't win the blue ribbon at the fair that Adams had counted on, and Gayle took the blame.

At school, though his I.Q. was rated as average and he "put out the utmost effort," it wasn't enough and he had to repeat subjects at summer school frequently in order to keep up with his class. His teachers called him a polite, cooperative, responsible boy, silent and hard to know, who just accepted the fact when he was a loser.

He took little interest in sports or school activities. He came to every school function, but "as a spectator not as a participant." This was in sharp contrast to his younger brother Lloyd, who had an infectious gayety and was in on everything, even to doing all the drawings for the school annual.

In 1942 Gayle went into the army for the first time and

was sent to the Pacific where he won his Bronze Star. When he was mustered out at the end of the war, he enrolled in the new Junior College set up for G.I.'s at Corsicana. Again he didn't do well, nor did he take part in campus life.

"He felt he was an outsider socially," one of his instructors said. "He got along well enough with his classmates though he wasn't popular and he had no girl. He was meek and quiet because he felt that was the role set for him. But he resented not having more, both financially and in ability to learn. He wanted to do well."

Although his grades were poor, under relaxed Texas requirements for returned veterans, Gayle went on with his studies at the University of Houston, taking one fall term and two summer sessions there and working as a lab assistant in chemistry. He failed most of his courses.

In the summer of 1948 he re-enlisted in the army and was sent overseas with the 24th Division, the first to land in Korea. Gayle was captured on New Year's Day, 1951, at the beginning of the second Chinese offensive.

He wrote letters home telling about how he had won a boxing match and had been given better clothes. He enclosed a picture of himself making a recorded propaganda broadcast for a Peiping radio station.

After hearing the broadcast repeated by local stations, Mrs. Adams wasn't "sure" that the voice was that of her son.

Two local boys who had known him in Corsicana and had been in prison camp with him as well both said he had been an early convert and there was no doubt that he was a progressive. Other prisoners of war said he seemed a much steadier, more earnest type than others of the twenty-one they had encountered.

A boy who went to school with him thought he had

"maybe kind of radical ideas but not Communist" before he went overseas.

"I don't know how to say it but he was just different than the others. He wasn't a mixer. He came out once for football, but that didn't last."

His father was sure his son was "just kidding the Reds. I have a feeling that he's just trying to outsmart them." His mother refused to comment.

"Like the rest," said Howard Gayle Adams as he prepared to go to China, "I am determined to fight for peace but I cannot fight for peace where there is no freedom of speech."

Cpl. Rufus Elbert Douglas

                           of Texon, Tex.

born March 21, 1927

                     re-enlisted March 19, 1949

2nd Division

                captured January 1, 1951

Protestant

            one semester college

average I.Q.

The Army Reported:

According to returned prisoners of war, Douglas wrote articles for the Communists, made propaganda broadcasts, read Communist books, attended classes organized for the study of Communism, and informed on his fellow prisoners. As a reward, he was given better living quarters and better food and was chosen as a member of a mess committee. The Chinese also showed their confidence in him by giving him other duties connected with recreation, mail and sanitation.

THERE WERE TEARS in the girl's eyes and she blinked to clear them away.

"We picked on him," she said. "We made fun of him. We just made life miserable for him. Why? I don't know. He was just a little old country boy and he didn't know how to act. It gets me now. If we had been a little nicer . . . if we had tried. . . ."

She didn't know it then but Rufus Elbert Douglas, who seemed to have been born to be bedeviled, was not to do any better in his new surroundings than he had done back home. For Douglas there is not even the remote possibility of a second chance. He will never come home again. The Chinese announced in June of 1954 that he had died of a "heart attack" somewhere in China.

There was no record of heart trouble of any sort in his medical history. It is unlikely that the true circumstances of his death will ever be known. But the conclusion is inescapable that the same qualities which caused him to be persecuted most of his life, qualities which made him fair game for the Reds, also made him most likely to get in trouble with his "hosts" behind the Iron Curtain.

Trouble dogged Elbert, as he was known growing up, from the time he was born. His father died when he was a baby. His mother remarried—unhappily. When he was eleven, she died too. His uncle and aunt, Mr. and Mrs. Ben

Howard, had promised her they'd take the boy and they did. They brought him to live with them in Texon, Tex., a dying company oil town on the edge of the west Texas fields.

Uncle Ben, who died while Elbert was overseas, was a tower man at the Texon fields. He worked nights and didn't see too much of his nephew—"He was either working or asleep," Mrs. Howard said—and the raising of her sister-in-law's boy fell to her.

"He didn't give me the trouble my own girls did," Mrs. Howard assured me as we sat on the low front steps of the cottage on the outskirts of San Angelo where she now lives. "I never had to spank him. My husband never did either, though he threatened to once because he wouldn't defend himself against the other kids when they picked on him. The only fights he ever got into was because he was scared of his uncle."

Elbert's mother, Frances Howard, never completely recovered from the effects of a childhood fever, Mrs. Howard said, and never quite "grew up." She married Elbert's father when she was in her teens. Left alone with a young baby, she remarried. This marriage was desperately unhappy and Elbert made plans as a child about how he would revenge himself when he was grown.

"He wouldn't talk much about his stepfather," Mrs. Howard said. "He did tell me about a time when his mother got the better of the man for once and was able to grab his wrists and push him back onto a red-hot stove. I knew his stepfather had beaten him too, but I got him to promise me he'd leave the man alone."

In a broadcast from Peiping after he went behind the Iron Curtain, Elbert spoke of how in those days he was so poor he used to "go to the bakery and ask for stale broken bread, unfit for sale."

"Elbert took after his mother," Mrs. Howard said. "He was a big boy, six foot two when he was nineteen, with brown hair and blue eyes. He was a real healthy boy, too. Oh, he had a little puny spell there for awhile but he wasn't ever really sick."

Texon, where the Howards lived when Elbert was growing up, sits drearily in the midst of a field of derricks—row on row of weatherbeaten company houses, grass growing bravely only in spots, trees stunted and wispy. The field is almost worked out now, but some wells are still pumping and fires, burning off the gas, flare here and there. The sulphur smell penetrates the area for miles around.

The town is off the highway and easy to miss unless you follow your nose. At the entrance is a sign: TEXON, PROPERTY OF THE BIG LAKE OIL COMPANY, WATCH OUT FOR CHILDREN.

Elbert couldn't play near home because his uncle was asleep daytimes. But he was a great help around the house, his aunt said.

"I taught him to do housework, just like the girls," she said, "and he thanked me for teaching him after he got in the army. He said it sure did come in handy when he had to go on KP duty.

"He was just as good a kid as you'd find. Never gave us a bit of trouble. He hated a fuss or trouble. If he thought I got upset or mad at him, or if he thought he had done something that would make me mad, he would walk the floor he would be so nervous."

Although his fellow students considered that he wasn't "sharp" in anything but mathematics, his grades were better than average up to high school, with even some A's. However, he was two years behind his age group when he came to Texon and he never made it up.

When he was sixteen he started taking the bus to the

161—

Reagan County Consolidated High School at Big Lake, thirteen miles away, the area's metropolis. If he had been picked on before, here he was really in for it with the more sophisticated town students.

One of his English teachers said he showed his resentment in class; that he was a boy it was hard to like, who didn't like either his teachers or his classmates and wasn't liked by them.

"He was persecuted in school," she said, "made fun of invariably. His personal appearance was against him; he was sloppy and his hair was never combed. Somewhere along the line he had been badly mistreated. He thought the teachers had it in for him and he would rebel. But while he was antagonistic, he wasn't forceful."

His grades were mixed at high school. He got B's in Math and Science and he flunked English. "He wouldn't even try in English," one classmate said.

His classmates in general felt that they hadn't known him and it was on their conscience that they hadn't tried. In defense they pointed out that Elbert himself didn't try to be close to anyone.

Only once did anyone remember him telling anything about his own life or his family. He was on the edge of a group that was discussing accidents.

"When I was little I fell out of a third-story window," he said, suddenly entering the conversation.

"How did it happen? Where was your mother?" they asked him.

"She was in a hospital with TB," he replied. "She died." There was a silence. No one knew what to say. Elbert shuffled away.

Just before his eighteenth birthday Elbert left school, his sophomore year not yet completed, to go into the army. That was the spring of 1945. World War II was still going on. He was discharged in December of 1946 and was the first of Reagan High's G.I.'s to return. He came back to school with advanced standing for maturity and experience in the army under Texas provisions for veterans. After attending for a year he went on, without a diploma, to Sul Ross State College in Alpine, Tex., under similar liberalized entrance requirements for veterans.

Elbert had played football for one season at Reagan—or most of one season. His coach said he was "one of those boys who is not with the group as a whole." He was quiet and reserved, "pretty aggressive at football but not one to go to extremes."

Classmates called him "big and clumsy," thought he had a "complex or something," maybe he was a little "shell-shocked" when he came back from the war.

"He felt left out of everything," said one, "and I guess he was. He didn't seem interested in girls. Didn't talk to them either."

But Bobby Reese, who spent a session with him at summer school making up part of the eighth grade, said he was "a good old boy, studied just enough to get along, but a steady boy." And parents of his contemporaries in Texon all called him a "nice quiet boy."

At Sul Ross State College, which in contrast to Texon is beautifully set in the mountains on the edge of the Big Bend country, Elbert stayed only one semester and is remembered but vaguely. He took three courses, flunked one, barely passed the other two. He gave up then and got taken on as a "roughneck" in the Odessa oil fields. The term covers a multitude of jobs, but Elbert most of the time drove a truck at $40 a week. After a short while he gave that up too and, without telling anyone, he re-enlisted in the army, in March of 1949. He went to Korea with the 2nd Division, was wounded in September of 1950, and was hardly back in the line before he was captured on New Year's Day, 1951, at the beginning of the second big Chinese offensive. He pleaded for letters from prison camp and although his aunt wrote him regularly, he didn't get but two of her letters. He was soon parroting the party line, particularly in the description of a holiday menu where he used the same adjectives describing a meal as those set out in a propaganda leaflet prepared by the Chinese People's Committee for World Peace. A copy of the leaflet was mailed to the San Angelo *Standard Times,* first in the country to receive one.

Before he left home, Elbert's interest in politics had been nonexistent; his ignorance of Communism vast. His letters were a puzzle to his aunt. They stopped coming just before he became one of the twenty-one. Mrs. Howard never gave up hope during the period the group was allowed for changing its mind.

She recorded a plea to be sent to him, describing the new house in San Angelo and how she was alone in it now that his uncle was dead. There was a lot of bad news that had to go into the recording. His half sister had died, too.

"Hi, son," Mrs. Howard started out. "It has been a long time since I saw you and I am sorry you didn't get my letters. Since you left your uncle has died and I am all alone here. . . . Elbert, I am sorry, but Alma is gone too. She went to California and got burned and passed away."

After listing the new babies born to his cousins, Mrs. Howard continued:

"Elbert, what took Uncle Ben was a cerebral hemorrhage. He had gone to work and he was sitting in his car by the doghouse and passed away as though he was asleep. He died at five in the afternoon and we didn't find him until 10:30. I laid him away in Rising Star Cemetery and someday I am going down there to live. I don't know yet. I sure am depending on you and hope you will come home soon.

"Alma was making a fire in California and the gas exploded, burning her awfully. I hope you get this real soon and will come home. I need you so bad."

Perhaps it was just as well that Elbert didn't hear that sad recital.

When correspondents were given a chance to question them en masse, the day before they left for China, Elbert had less to say than most of the twenty-one, but it was out of the same copybook:

"I want to fight for world peace, too. But it is not possible in the U. S. That was proved by what happened to Dickenson."

Before leaving Texon, I talked to an oil field roughneck about Elbert. He squinted to that horizon interlaced with derricks as far as the eye could see and kicked at a clod. The smell of sulphur and the dust assailed your nostrils and clogged your throat.

"If anybody over there treated that boy decently," he said, "I don't blame him for staying. He sure never got a bit of good treatment here." Nor there, either, in the end.

Pfc. Lewis W. Griggs

of Neches, Tex.

born August 2, 1932

enlisted August 4, 1949

25th Division

captured April 25, 1951

Baptist

2 years high school

average I.Q.

The Army Reported:

According to returned prisoners, Griggs wrote articles for Chinese publications, tried to influence other prisoners by preaching Communism, circulated and signed peace petitions and voluntarily made propaganda recordings. He was an informer *who collaborated with the Chinese in every way that would ingratiate himself to them. He was appointed to membership on a "peace committee."*

N<small>ECHES</small>, <small>TEX</small>., is a tiny farm community 120 miles from Dallas on U. S. 79. Just before you reach it the plains give way to unexpected hills and trees provide a welcome shade. Its main street is the highway. The railroad station is on one side and the general store and a few houses on the other. A road behind the store leads up a gentle rise which you learn is known locally as "the mountain."

"Turn left and then you go all the way to the top of the mountain and the house will be on the right." I drove six miles looking for the mountain before I turned back and found it right behind the store.

It's a small frame house—the farm—where Lewis W. Griggs lived before he went into the army. It has a sign on it now: <small>PRIVATE PROPERTY—NOT FOR SALE—KEEP OFF</small>.

Lewis' father was an electrician, "did right well; worked for wages." He died while his son was in prison camp. Mrs. Griggs works as a practical nurse and lives in nearby Jacksonville with her remaining son.

Mention Lewis Griggs in Neches and they shake their heads. "He was a strange one," a neighbor reiterated. "He stood aloof. Didn't speak if he didn't care to. Town like this everyone knows everyone else. Speaks to everyone else. But he'd just go along with his head in the air. Wouldn't speak. Wouldn't even look at you.

"Well, now, maybe it wasn't my place, but I used to speak to him anyway, just to try to get him to talk."

As in many rural communities, most of the young people who were children here with Lewis have scattered and gone. Those that remain remember him as a "lone wolf."

"He didn't mix much with the other kids," one girl said. "His father was strict with him. Only place he could go was to church. He just wasn't like the rest of us."

The rural high school at Neches was consolidated with the city high school at Palestine and Lewis rode the bus eighteen miles to attend what turned out to be his last school session.

He was sixteen, big for his age, six foot two, and he played on the football squad, made the B team and got a letter. He got an 82 in algebra but barely passed his other courses, including a special course in U. S. and Texas Constitution, which is necessary for graduation.

"He had a nice smile but you seldom saw it," one teacher said. "He was a peculiar boy," said another.

Most teachers remembered him only vaguely but there was one who remembered him very well and thinks that "we didn't do everything we could have.

"He seemed to be a boy you couldn't reach," she said. "He was quiet, withdrawn, polite and bored. He was just there. He didn't do his work. He just came and that's all. He sat in the back of the room and I gave him an opportunity to move up front but he didn't want to. It would make him too prominent.

"He was physically mature for his age, not at all boyish. He came in and left the building not as a high school boy, but as a man. He gave me the feeling as I watched him from day to day that he felt this was all unnecessary. When I called on him he would give me a surprised look as if to say, 'Why is she bothering me?'

—170

"He looked out of his eyes as if he had the weight of the world on him. I felt sorry for him; I wished I could do something for that boy.

"Perhaps I could have done something. Perhaps if I had given him some responsibility, he might have responded."

Although Lewis' family was considered well-off in Neches —his father "worked for wages"—in the affluent town of Palestine, he was thought of as an underprivileged "rural" child. The town and rural children seldom mix well in these consolidated schools, and Lewis was no mixer anyway. He was never seen with anyone else around the halls of the school; "he never paid the slightest attention to girls in class or in the corridors."

He was absent a good deal from classes and after an incident on the school bus where some of the other students picked on him and teased him—no one remembers why or what about—he left high school. His family sent him to nearby Allen Military Academy, but he left there at the end of six weeks. The day after his seventeenth birthday he enlisted in the army.

Lewis became a stretcher bearer in a medical company in the 35th Regiment of the 25th Infantry which landed in Korea on July 13, 1950. His company took much of the brunt of the first North Korean victories and fought its way up toward the Yalu River when the tide was turned. It was in the disastrous withdrawal that came with the Chinese entry into the field. Lewis was captured April 25, 1951, when the United Nations forces were about to repulse the last major Chinese attack.

Palestine High School knew that Lewis had become a progressive. He wrote a letter addressed to the principal, D. N. Stewart, and the students of the school:

I am writing to you and the student body to urge your fullest cooperation in striving for a peaceful settlement of the Korean conflict. Do you realize that for the length of the Korean war, so referred to as a "police action," has caused the U. S. more casualties than a like period in World War II? Can the American people allow such a war as this to continue without putting out a strong effort to stop it?

No one at Palestine thought that Lewis Griggs had written the letter.

"It's not the way an East Texas country boy from the red clay hills would write," they said.

His mother, a tall, spare woman with large, haunted blue eyes, has not talked about Lewis since he went behind the Iron Curtain January 28, 1954.

"I just don't want to discuss it," she said. "I don't want to be rude but I don't want to talk about it."

Earlier, she had told how her son had begged his parents to let him join the army, until they finally permitted him to when he was only seventeen. She refused to believe that he had become a Communist of his own will.

"He is only twenty-one," she said. "For the life of me I cannot understand it. Lewis loved his home and his country and if we can ever get him home I think we can all understand it. He wasn't brought up to be a Communist. He was raised in a Christian home. He was a member of the Baptist Church. He declared himself at a revival meeting in California before he went overseas. I believe he may have been forced to do this. All I want is to get him back home. I want to ask people to be patient with these boys so that when we can get them back home, they will change, if they ever have changed. I don't believe my boy is a Communist or has any Communistic leanings."

Later, Mrs. Griggs accused the Communists of using narcotics to distort her son's mind.

"I work in a hospital and I see every day how people react under the combination of fear and narcotics," she said.

There had been no letters from Lewis for over a year.

"After his father died, I wrote and told him I was going to sell the farm, but he wrote back and asked me to keep it for him until he got home. I can't believe he isn't coming home," she said.

Mrs. Griggs was one of the many mothers who hoped that she would be able to go over to Korea and talk to her boy herself. "I have confidence in the leaders we are sending to the Neutral Zone to talk to those boys, but if a mother can't touch her boy's heart, I don't know who can. The shock of the mothers showing up there could be effective. . . . I'd like to take my hands and put them on my boy's head and hold his face in my hands. I don't believe my boy has turned Communist. He was a good, sweet boy and there's nothing wrong with him that couldn't be straightened out if he could come back home."

Returned prisoners of war who were in Camp III with Griggs are not so sure. "He was a peculiar egg," said one. "I felt kind of sorry for him," said another, "in spite of everything. I don't think he was quite right."

Just before he left for China with the rest of the twenty-one, Griggs made the usual statement:

"My reason is very simple. No one can speak up for peace in a nation where the government is run by people like McCarthy, McCarran and Smith."

Pfc. Morris R. Wills

        of West Fort Ann, N. Y.

born May 3, 1933

        enlisted July 27, 1950

2nd Division

        captured May 18, 1951

Protestant

        2 years high school

I.Q. 106

The Army Reported:

According to returned prisoners of war, Wills was active in Communist study groups, circulated peace petitions, made propaganda recordings for broadcast, and tried to persuade fellow prisoners to accept Communism. His rewards from the Communists included much attention and many favors and a large degree of freedom.

Two boys in uniform showed up at the Fort Ann High School dance in the fall of 1950, shortly after they had left school, shortly before they were to go to Korea.

"We had to ask them to leave," an instructor said regretfully, "because they had been drinking. They protested. They said they might never come back. And it almost came true for both of them."

One was severely wounded—and one was Morris Wills of West Fort Ann, N. Y., who stayed with the enemy and will never come back.

Village folk and farmers in this upland dairy community in the foothills of the Adirondacks were puzzled when they heard that one of their lads was among the twenty-one who refused repatriation. They were shocked when they saw Morris on television the day the group left for the interior of China.

"He didn't look like himself." . . . "He was awfully fat." . . . "He seemed so nervous, pacing back and forth behind the others." . . . "His eyes—he looked like a lost soul."

No one could explain why Morris should have been one of the twenty-one. Teachers and townsfolk alike had considered him a pretty average kid, bright enough, good-looking enough, likable enough, if easily led and somewhat reticent and ingrown.

They didn't know that the farm boy had fallen in love

177—

with a Chinese nurse, daughter of a Communist general, while he was sick in a prison hospital and had married her. He didn't write about it in his letters home.

It is an interesting point that the three big crises in Morris' life had turned on illness. When he was three he had been rushed to the hospital with a burst appendix. His mother felt that he had had a close brush with death and worried that he would not recover. From then until he went to school she kept him at her side, took him wherever she went, leaving even the younger children at home.

Then when he was eleven, his mother became seriously ill. She died a year later of cancer. Her death had a profound effect on the boy. His record in school which up until then had been better than average started to go down. He was restless at home and when his uncle, who had no sons, asked him to come down and stay with his family and do the chores, he agreed.

He spent about two years at his uncle's farm—the next one down the road from the home farm—going up Sundays to be with his own brothers and sisters. His uncle, Jay Gilmore, is dead now. His aunt Katherine is annoyed at current gossip that the two quarreled.

"They never did," she told me. "Wouldn't either one of them say nothing if they were mad so they couldn't hardly quarrel. If Morris didn't like a thing you wouldn't know it. He never was impudent or talked back. Nobody could get to him; he was kind of all by himself. Maybe he was more sensitive than we knew."

His aunt thought that Morris had enlisted because he didn't want to go to school, "but if the truth was known I'd say when the day came to go into the army he didn't want to any more."

Morris had been pretty close to his mother, Mrs. Gilmore

—178

agreed. "She ruled them all up there. And he was stubborn all right, like she was. But he did the chores pretty good. And he was a bright boy. Never brought a book home or studied while he was here, but he passed everything just the same."

An old friend of the family remembers how Mrs. Wills came to see them shortly after Morris' younger sister was born and how annoyed her mother was "because she wanted to hold the new baby and she brought Morris instead."

"Bessie Wills was a strong-minded woman," another old friend said. "She ruled the roost and I guess she needed to with them six younguns. But she was sure set on little Morris. He was the apple of her eye."

"Yes, he was Mama's favorite," his older sister Muriel, who has run the home since her mother's death, agreed. Muriel remembers Morris as a precocious child who walked at nine months and talked when he was a year old. He had asthma as a child and "might have felt misunderstood," she says, "but he never showed his feelings except to sulk.

"He used to help Mama around the house, but after she died I never liked to ask him to do anything."

Farm distances being what they are he had few playmates his own age when he was small. But he had a dog named Skipper. Growing up, his life was little different from that of the other farm boys in the area.

When he got old enough he had a gun and went shooting rabbits or hunting deer in the hills or fishing in the streams and lakes. He didn't take part in school athletics or any other school activities but he lived four miles away and had chores to do after school.

Fort Ann, about seventy-five miles north of Albany near the Vermont border, is a Main Street town which supplies the dairy farmers of the surrounding countryside. It is part of the milk shed for the New York City area. There is little diversified farming. The farms range from shacks on a few acres of scrub to completely mechanized outfits on lush bottomland. The Wills farm lies in between these extremes. Jake Wills, Morris' father, adds to the income by supervising the county roads. Morris and his father had never been close. When William, the oldest son, took over the farm management a few years ago, some of the townspeople believe that Morris felt left out.

The family is Protestant, but not much on churchgoing; Morris seldom went himself. On his last day to make a choice, his sister went to the local Roman Catholic church to pray for him, though the family had never attended there before.

At home the rules were strict. Morris had never had a drink before he went into uniform and showed up at the high school dance. When asked if his questions on sex had been answered, Muriel said, "We wouldn't have dared ask any such questions."

Morris wanted desperately to get away from the farm. His ambitions, the same as many boys his age in the community, were to quit school, get a job, get a car—in that order.

"You see, these boys learn to drive a tractor before they are twelve," a high school teacher told me. "So far as the mechanical part goes they know how to drive perfectly. They can't understand why they couldn't have a car. And some of them do. We had an eighth grader who drove himself to and from school every day."

With Morris the urge to drive, coupled with the wish to get away from the farm, grew so strong that it got him in his one brush with the authorities.

Five or six local boys, Morris among them, had worked out plans over a period of months to get a car and go to California. All but one of the others dropped out at the end and Morris would have too except that he was taunted as "chicken" and took the dare.

They took a jalopy belonging to the other boy's father, loaded it up with food, blankets and their guns and started off on their transcontinental tour. It ended abruptly less than a hundred miles from home when the car, of antique vintage, broke down near Albany and the two were picked up by state troopers and taken to jail.

The boys were not charged and were released to their fathers. The incident, however, had only increased Morris' determination to get away from home and school. Finally, two months after he was seventeen, he persuaded his father to sign for his enlistment a month after the Korean fracas started.

Morris was not the only Fort Ann boy to go into the army that year and the next. Some of the others got to Korea, too. The rest came back, some to their farm homes and some to take jobs in nearby "big towns."

I tried to see them. The first one had gone hunting that morning. The second one had gone to Albany. The third one careened out of the farm road just as I was about to turn into it. The others just weren't around and nobody could say when they would be around. I tried again the next day with similar results. Then a storekeeper who had given me directions wised me up.

"News travels fast around here," he said. "Everybody knows you're asking about Morris Wills. Kids around here stick together and they don't talk. Maybe they didn't like Morris, or maybe they did. Maybe they didn't approve of what he did. But they just aren't going to talk to a stranger about him when they won't even talk about him with their folks."

When I finally cornered one of them, I learned how right my storekeeper friend was.

"I'll talk to you if you won't use my name," he said, after his pretty young wife persuaded him to at least see me. "But I haven't got anything to say," he added with patent embarrassment. "I just don't want to talk about him, one way or the other. But I just don't know how anyone, even if he didn't get past first grade, would be fool enough to stay and eat rice with those gooks with all the money he had coming to him."

Then, realizing he had said more than he had meant to, he hurried out of the house, saying over his shoulder as he left, "I'm late already. I've got to go now."

Morris got to Korea after the Chinese had shown their full strength, as a replacement in the badly mauled 2nd Division. He was captured May 18, 1951, during the spring offensive.

His letters home were called "phony" by his father. His family were sure it wasn't his handwriting.

"It is my understanding," one letter went, "that there is a peace movement back there, so tell Father that with all my heart I hope he supports the peace movement to his fullest ability in faith that it will bring me back home, quick and safe."

Muriel said that he had never called his father anything but "Dad." The letter spoke of harvesting wheat and of the "hired man." There is no wheat and no hired man.

"I am well and all right over here," he added, "except for one thing. The days are long and hot and tiresome and I keep longing for the day when I can return home safely."

That day didn't come for Morris Wills.

"People who voice an opinion for peace in the United States," he said after the last day had come and gone when he could return home safely, "are persecuted and their voices suppressed. There is not a democratic government in the United States as long as McCarthyism and McCarranism are allowed to exist. The people will not be allowed to fight for peace. There is no freedom of speech."

He indicated that he, like the leader of the group, Richard Corden, was "hopeful of becoming a Communist."

"He must have been afraid to come—or they wouldn't let him," said his aunt.

"I can't think why he would do it," said the mother of one of his friends, "unless his mind went bad."

A high school teacher who had pondered his case long and thoughtfully felt that Morris had lacked "guts," was the kind of boy who would be easily led, who always "knuckled under," and would give up when the odds were too great.

Pvt. Richard R. Tenneson

        of Alden, Minn.

born June 4, 1933

        enlisted July, 1950

2nd Division

        captured May 18, 1951

Baptist

        3rd year high school

high I.Q.

The Army Reported:

According to returned prisoners of war, Tenneson collaborated with Communist officials, informed on fellow prisoners, circulated petitions, attended special study classes, made propaganda recordings for broadcast, attempted to convert fellow prisoners to Communism, and consistently supported the Communist propaganda program. His rewards included liquor and marijuana.

"I GOT NO HOME," said the stocky seventeen-year-old in uniform, on his last leave before going into the fighting in Korea. "You'll never see me again."

It is doubtful that Richard Tenneson really thought his dark prophecy would be fulfilled. He couldn't have known that three years later he would be exchanging the rolling plains around Alden, Minn., for the alien vistas of Communist China.

All of his life Richard had swung like a pendulum between schools, between religions, between homes. Even in prison he vacillated at first between being a "progressive" as those who lined up with the Reds were called and being a "reactionary" as those who resisted were called.

In the end he got caught on a downswing that never came up—caught so fast that in December of 1953 he sat in the neutral compound in Panmunjom and composed a rude and jeering letter to his mother. He didn't do it all by himself. He got a lot of help from his twenty-one companion prisoners of war who were refusing to return to home and country.

As each sentence was polished off, it was read aloud to be criticized or applauded by the group. When it was finished all were childishly pleased with the results.

And in a hotel room in Tokyo, a woman who had come halfway around the world in the forlorn hope of talking her son out of his fateful decision, read the letter and wept.

"United States authorities . . . have probably told you that I was forced, doped, brainwashed or some other horse manure that they use to slander and defile people like myself who will stand up for his own rights and the rights of man," the letter said. "As soon as you read this you had better go over to GHQ and take a loyalty oath or you are likely to be arraigned before the House of Un-American Activities." (The misphrasing is in the letter.)

After that Mrs. Portia Howe gave up trying to get permission of the army to go to Korea and see her son in person.

"I have failed somewhere," she said then, "and I must find out where, because I have three other children. I believe a mother should start at birth trying to train a child for life. Perhaps I overdid it. Richard resented discipline. Perhaps that is where I made my mistake."

It wasn't as simple as that. If Richard's trouble was discipline it was too many different disciplines rather than too much. He never had a settled home, nor went to the same school for any length of time. He was even baptized into three different churches.

He lived with his grandmother during his pre-school years and after, lived a few months with one aunt, a year with another. As a baby he was baptized a Lutheran, his father's religion; when he was six he was baptized a Catholic; when he was thirteen, a Baptist.

He went to school at Clark's Grove, then Alden, then New Richland, then Albert Lea, then back to Alden—all towns in southern Minnesota.

His father and mother were divorced when he was two years old. His mother remarried when he was eight and he never accepted his stepfather.

During his growing-up period, Richard was under the influence of two remarkable women, his mother and his grandmother. Mother and daughter resemble one another in an unusual degree in looks, manner and character. Mrs. Howe, a much handsomer woman than her photographs would suggest, might be ten years younger than forty-three, her actual age; her mother, Mrs. John W. Jensen, looks twenty years younger than seventy. Both are strong and erect, both look at you directly out of large, clear, dark eyes. Both are well read, thoughtful, aware of current intellectual trends—and both are religious fanatics.

To Mrs. Jensen one of the "most heartbreaking times" in her life was "when my daughter became a Catholic."

"It was at the time of Nathan's birth," Mrs. Jensen added. "A Catholic family befriended her." She turned her direct gaze on me. "I don't know what your religion is or whether you've been born again, but at that time my daughter had not been born again; she hadn't had the real experience with religion. She wanted to be right with God and there was this very efficient priest and he won out enough to get both boys baptized Catholics."

After his mother married Ebenezer Howe in 1941, in a Methodist ceremony, Richard stopped going to the Catholic church and when he was thirteen he was baptized in the Baptist church by a minister who did not know of the previous baptismal records.

"Religion was never a happy thing in Richard's family," one of his many pastors told me. "In addition the boy had a sense of not belonging anywhere. He went from home to home, never quite having a real home. He had to be pretty careful how he handled himself."

Portia Jensen and Russell Tenneson were married in June of 1932 and a year later Richard was born. Sickly at birth he was soon a healthy, sturdy baby who could be left

with his grandmother when his parents struck out for Min-
neapolis in search of work at the depth of the depression.
Tenneson had been a truck driver and a garage mechanic
but found it hard to get a job. His wife sold cosmetics door
to door and did fairly well. But something went wrong with
their marriage and Mrs. Tenneson got a divorce on charges
of abandonment and desertion in the summer of 1935.

Mrs. Tenneson came back to home territory and worked
as a housekeeper and waitress. During the years when she
had to make her own living, Richard stayed with his grandparents most of the time.

"I think myself," Mrs. Jensen said, "that we talked out of
turn about his father in front of him. You know my father
died when I was a baby and Mother told us only wonderful
things about him. But death is a clean thing and divorce is
different and we talked out of turn."

Mrs. Jensen said that Richard was a bright child from
the beginning but he stayed off from other children "just
like his mother did." As a baby he had an allergy to cream
but recovered from it. The children in the neighborhood
picked on him because he wore a snowsuit and the rest
didn't, his grandmother remembered.

"But when things didn't suit him, he could go it alone,"
Mrs. Jensen said. "He could take a lot of punishment. Once
he ran away and slept on a bench in a park. He was about
fifteen then. He'd heard us tell about how his father ran
away when he was that age."

Mrs. Howe married her present husband, Ebenezer K.
Howe, in 1941 and they came to the farm near Alden where
the family now lives. Neighbors and teachers all remarked
on Richard's difficulties with his stepfather. On the back of
his card at Albert Lea High School was the notation that he

was living with an aunt that year because he "couldn't get along with stepfather."

Freeborn County, where Rick Tenneson lived most of his life, is almost completely rural. Albert Lea, the biggest town in the area, named for an army surveyor, has a population of less than fourteen thousand; Clark's Grove and Alden are tiny hamlets. The farms he lived on were distant even from these centers.

Teachers, neighbors and classmates all have different slants on Richard. Some consider him just a "normal, average kid." Some say he was bull-headed and hard to get along with. Most said he didn't mix much with other boys or date girls at all. One classmate told a teacher before Richard's name was announced as one of the group: "If anyone would fall for the Communist line, Richard would."

L. J. Adolphsen, principal of the Albert Lea High School, doesn't remember him—"Nothing about him stood out"—but noted that the physical education people found him surly. He came and went on the school bus and took no part in extracurricular activities either there or at Alden High School.

An Indian guard at the neutral camp said Richard told him he had been picked on at home because he was undersized and not good at sports.

A teacher told me that "he never really had a home or any stable environment—just an overload of sin and save the world."

The Howes themselves are controversial figures in the community. Some neighbors blamed them because Richard had signed a petition in his last year in high school seeking the ouster of a school official. Several expressed the feeling that Richard's parents should have taught him "more respect for his teachers." They felt that Mrs. Howe was "pretty opinionated."

The community was divided when Mrs. Howe determined that she would go to Korea and attempt to talk her son out of his fearful decision. Circulars were placed in every mailbox asking contributions to help defray the high costs of the flight to the Orient. Only a little more than $200 was raised and Mrs. Howe had to cash in the bonds Richard sent home to manage her expenses.

Despite the difficulties in the way, difficulties which proved insurmountable to all of the other mothers who tried, Mrs. Howe got as far as Tokyo in her vain attempt to get Rick to come home. Her first major victory was scored when after a two-hour conference she persuaded Mrs. Ruth B. Shipley, watchdog of the passport division of the State Department, to give her the necessary credentials to get as far as Japan.

The Howe farmhouse is a comfortable one, set up on a rise above the road. The Howes have developed a successful business in dressed poultry, selling direct to the consumer. The house was filled with the tantalizing aroma of freshly baked bread the day I stopped there. The ten-year-old twins, Ebenezer, Jr., and Jan, were doing their homework at one end of the living room as I talked to Mrs. Howe. She was pleasant and courteous but obviously taut and under a strain.

She sees her son as a boy who got along normally with his brothers and sister, was well adjusted, who could play by himself when he needed to, who changed his friends as he himself progressed—"a boy with a wonderful imagination who could have a perfectly wonderful time imagining things and playing by himself."

She thought perhaps they had expected too much of him "in certain areas as most parents do," but she did not think

—192

he had been punished excessively and he was "not usually" spanked.

At that one of the twins, Ebenezer, Jr., piped up:

"All right, do you remember the time daddy went after him with the horsewhip?"

"Yes," Mrs. Howe said calmly, "but that was because he left the milking machine on the cow and it hurt the cow."

Richard's main ambition was for "maturity," Mrs. Howe felt. "He wanted to grow up." He was a great reader and he had thought of being a teacher or a doctor.

When he was sixteen, Richard got a job with a traveling carnival and got in his only difficulties with the police when one of his carnival acquaintances stole a car and took him along on a wild ride toward Fort Riley, Kansas, where Richard was going to enlist. They were picked up in Nebraska and Mrs. Howe had to come and get him. Richard was charged with juvenile delinquency and given a suspended sentence.

When he was just over seventeen and the Korean war had been on a few weeks, Richard finally did enlist. He left with his last year in high school yet to go. His school record had been spotty though his I.Q. was high. He was crazy to get into the army, his mother said, and he pointed out he could go to college under the G.I. Bill and he would be drafted eventually anyway. So Mrs. Howe signed for his enlistment.

He came back on his last leave in February of 1951, before he was sent to the battle lines. That was when he told his friend, "I got no home." And that was when he told his mother:

"If I should win the Congressional Medal of Honor, I still wouldn't have done enough for my country."

Richard was reported missing in action on May 18, 1951, just a few weeks after he went into the line. This was during the second attack of the Chinese Communist spring offensive and the already battered 2nd Division, Richard's outfit, took the brunt of it.

"He began to swallow the Commie line right after he was captured," a fellow prisoner of war who didn't, told me. "He was always talking about Communism. He liked to talk about it. He knew a lot about it because he studied the Reds' propaganda. We would ask him why he came to Korea to fight and he would say he didn't know the real story until the Chinese told him."

Still, he just missed being saved. His bunkmates included a group of airborne troops who had banded together to counteract the effects of the Red propaganda.

"We had him all talked out of it," Charles Loutitt of Monongahela, Pa., who won a Bronze Star for his heroism in prison camp, told me. "But then the Communists broke us up and sent us to other camps and we lost him."

Lost him so far that he was listed as an informer by the army which also accused him of making propaganda recordings for broadcast in return for liquor and marijuana.

Fellow prisoners suspected him of reporting them to the Chinese and threatened him several times.

"I got fed up," one said, "and asked him to step outside. He refused to fight. It was just as well because hitting a progressive meant being put in a cage or on hard labor."

Tenneson was one of the ones the Communists counted on as a leader of the group. In spite of the legal difficulties in the way of allowing his mother to come to the camp, our officials were seriously considering how her visit could be made possible until they got word that an unhappy incident —the nature of it was never known—was being planned by the group should she make her appearance.

The joint letter sent out under Richard's signature was

—194

confirmation enough that Mrs. Howe's visit to Korea might do more harm than good.

The letter started out "Dear Mother" but it closed with no protestations of love, only this: "Say hello to the family if you are not allowed to come and see me" and then his signature.

However, in the body of the letter he insisted that he still loved "my family, my people and my country and whether you are able to understand or not, believe me when I say it is for them I am fighting and it is impossible for me to live in the United States because I want to live as I wish."

In another part, he declared that "during life I have witnessed both peace and war in the United States. I love peace. I love mankind. I love them enough to fight for them. That is what I am doing now—that is why I am not going home."

Through her tears, Mrs. Howe said hopelessly to Tokyo correspondents:

"What does he know of life in the United States? He was in combat seven weeks. What does he know of war?"

He described life in the camp "in the Democratic People's Republic of Korea" as a "lot of fun" with sports, folk dancing, "cultural concerts" and the prospect of ice skating over the flooded rice fields.

He asked her to pay a visit to the Japanese wife of Claude Batchelor, "one of my friends," whose name he misspelled, to ask her to write her husband and try to get permission to visit him. Just before she left for home, her mission unaccomplished, Mrs. Howe did pay a visit to Kiyoko Araki whose letters, written shortly afterward, were credited with persuading Batchelor to leave the camp just before the deadline.

For Batchelor this was not a return to freedom. He was

sentenced to life imprisonment, later reduced to twenty years, by a court-martial. Mrs. Howe attended, "so that I can see what I may be up against some day."

Of her own son, she said she did not believe that "very much in Richard's background" had anything to do with where he is.

"I don't believe that anyone brought up as Richard was could be happy under Communist rule. I am depending on the Lord to show him how wrong the Communists are."

A letter she received from her son in August suggested he might have found out a few things, at least that he was homesick. Mrs. Howe sent him some family pictures and he received them. In reply he sent a picture of himself and of part of the group. He wrote: "It is hard to explain how I felt when I saw your picture. It makes me sad at times to think that we can't be together now."

He also wrote the twins warning them "to pay attention" in school because "if you know a lot nobody can cheat you."

And to Nathan, the brother closest to him in age who was captain of the 1954 football team at Alden High School, he wrote the most poignant, revealing letter of all.

Every night I look at your picture and I feel remorseful. What more can I say?

Don't leave home yet. . . . You don't know the security that home offers until you are away from it. How important education is you realize after the lack of it has led you into a blind alley. Don't join the armed forces yet.

Unfortunately for Richard, he has already reached the end of his blind alley and if he has found out how badly he has been cheated by the Communists, it no longer can help. He is caught in the web.

—196

Pfc. John R. Dunn

of Baltimore, Md.

born June 27, 1928

drafted December 12, 1950

2nd Division

captured July 24, 1951

Episcopal

high school grad

average I.Q.

The Army Reported:

According to returned prisoners of war, Dunn became a lecturer for the Communists, wrote articles for the Communist Daily Worker *of London, made special studies of Communism, collaborated with camp officials and attempted to convert his fellow prisoners. He was a member of the "Kremlin Club" and his rewards included appointment as camp librarian.*

F OR THE *Green Bag,* yearbook of Baltimore's City College which, despite its name, is a high school, John Roedel Dunn declared that it was his ambition "to be happy." While that is a normal enough human ambition it is seldom expressed in high school annuals and John Dunn was the only one to put it down in 1948.

On the surface, his chances of achieving it seemed good. A handsome, serious-faced boy, always well dressed and immaculate, he had earned the respect of his pastor—"One of the finest boys I know"—and his employer. He was looked up to by his pretty sister and his younger brother. His family was well-off; his father personnel director of a big industrial firm; his mother also employed by a wholesale grocery company.

Why then should he have chosen to collaborate with his captors and refuse repatriation to his own country?

There are no simple answers and this one is further complicated by the conflicting reports of fellow prisoners of war who did return.

"Don't believe a thing you hear," one wrote his parents, Mr. and Mrs. William Dunn. "Don't believe a word you read. Jack's a good boy. I refuse to believe it."

Alfred Graham, Jr., from his hospital bed in St. Albans, was more specific:

"Dunn gave me his blanket and his ration of sugar when I was sick on the thirty-one-day march north to the Yalu

River," Graham said. "He waited on me hand and foot. He treated others in the company like that, too. Jack was in no way a progressive as I should know because I became his closest friend. He was very popular; the whole company liked him. He was kind and he was a good person—just good."

Pose those against this:

"He was filthy; the dirtiest guy in camp. We threw him in the river once as the only way to clean him up. The others didn't want to have anything to do with him."

Or this:

"He was a tagger. If there was anything going on, Dunn wanted to get in on it, whatever it was. He tried to talk like a college professor and was always haranguing the guys who wouldn't turn progressive."

Which is right? Both.

The glowing reports come from Dunn's stay in Prison Camp III where he spent the first year of his imprisonment. The critical ones are from prisoners of war who knew him in Camp V where he made his decision not to return to his own country.

Exact details of what happened to him between the two camps will never be known. But there are definite clues to the puzzle of how a youth of his background and training could have become one of the twenty-one.

John was born in Altoona, Pa., June 27, 1928, the oldest of three children. The Dunn family had many connections in Altoona, spreading through all social levels, and the William Dunns were well known and well liked in the community. They shared the hard times of the depression which struck Altoona with particular force. Still, his father, starting as a clerk, worked up to assistant personnel manager. When John was thirteen, the job in Baltimore opened up and the family moved there.

John R. Dunn

John is remembered, if at all, by neighbors and teachers in Altoona as a quiet, shy boy. He repeated first grade, but the teacher who would know why is now dead. His grades were poor and when he transferred to Baltimore he repeated half of the seventh grade and became a midyear student.

He was given I.Q. tests four different times, receiving grades as low as 93 and as high as 111, an unusually wide variance (100 is average).

He was almost seventeen when he entered the junior year in Baltimore's City College, a high school with traditions reaching back more than two hundred years, which specialized in classical studies as against the technical high schools in the city.

John didn't take the classical course but a sort of hybrid technical course for students without the interest or qualifications for either classical or advanced technical studies.

He was in a room that was classified as a mixed low-average group of "indifferent" students.

"They took courses to avoid taking other courses," one teacher said. "They did not get a cultural background making for a well-rounded life. They had a vague feeling that they were not being treated as well as the others."

In this group John stood out because of his appearance— he was always neat and well dressed—because of his age and because of his "high ideals." He "achieved the respect" of his classmates and was chosen by them to be home room president in his senior year.

In the meantime John, who had been a regular churchgoer most of his life, began to take an unusual interest in the Episcopal Church of the Resurrection in the northern part of Baltimore which his family now attended.

"He hovered around the church most of his life," said the Reverend Elmer P. Baker. "I wish I had a dozen like him."

The church lost its sexton and John took his place as an unpaid volunteer, cleaning and painting and fixing up everything that needed attending to. He would come directly from school every afternoon, spending all his free time at the church.

"He loved his church," the Reverend Baker said. "He was in and out of here all the time. My wife and I thought the world of him. He was cheerful, cooperative, dependable. If he undertook to do anything, you could forget it. He would do it."

This was quite at variance with his record at school. The teacher who best remembers him recalls that he was "shy and sensitive, physically frail, indifferent to school, uninterested in sports or extracurricular activities, with no particular pals; his grades were low."

But he tended a cottage colony of summer camps in his vacations and did it well; after graduation from high school he got a job as a route man for his mother's company, selling potato chips and cookies around Baltimore on commission, and did well at that too.

He continued to spend his free time around the church, took part in all the young people's organizations and became assistant superintendent of the Sunday School. But he never had a date with a girl.

Like most of the twenty-one, John was the oldest boy in the family. He got along well with his only brother Bill, who was about two years younger, despite their obvious temperamental differences. They were never known to quarrel; though Bill was quite a scrapper away from home, John was not. They did a good many things together, particularly in their younger days. Bill was interested in the church but not to the degree that John was, although the two always decorated the church Christmas tree together.

Their paths diverged notably as they got up in their teens. Then Bill outstripped his older brother in size. He had an easy way with his own age group; took part in all the normal activities of a teenager, going to dances and parties while John stayed home or went over to the church; and eventually courting and marrying the girl next door.

There was something wrong through all this time. John wasn't well. He had had asthma and hay fever when he was younger. In his teens he began having severe headaches and unexplained blackouts and fainting spells. His family took him from doctor to doctor with no results. Finally they took him to a psychiatrist. His report remains secret.

When John was twenty-two, the draft call came. (He is the only draftee of the twenty-one.) The Korean war had already started. John came to his pastor to talk it over with him. He told Dr. Baker that he was willing to go in and get it over with and thought he should because "I am in a better position than some; I have no responsibilities."

His acceptance by the medical board came as a surprise to those close enough to him to know his medical history. Still, army life seemed to agree with him. "He looked well when he came back to Baltimore on leave," Dr. Baker said.

However, on the transport going over to Tokyo, the medical officer who examined him said, "I don't know how you got in but I can tell you you're going back as soon as we get over." He was wrong. It didn't happen that way. John Dunn was put in the battle line as a radioman in June of 1951 and in July he was captured.

Fellow prisoners said he was captured because he stayed to take care of a seriously wounded officer who could not attempt to escape when the unit was surrounded by Chinese and North Koreans. The officer was shot by his captors. On the long, hard march north to the Yalu River prison camps, others died too, including one of John's pals.

Word that he was among the group that would refuse to be repatriated was a complete shock to his family and friends —something almost too hard to take in. Letters from prison camp had contained no hint even that he had begun to collaborate.

"You could always depend on Jack, like you could on your clock," his mother said.

"My older brother made me and Bill toe the line in our teenage days," said his pretty blonde sister Barbara.

"If a brilliant and dedicated man like Cardinal Mindszenty can be made to confess crimes, what chance has a G.I.?" said his father.

Governor McKeldin of Maryland made a personal appeal to the youth in a recorded message, asking him "to renounce Communism and return to his home and family.

"Come home, John," he said, "come home to the freedom and dignity of America. The United States has no imperialist ambitions. It is the Communists who are the would-be conquerors of the world."

The Governor went on to describe the beauty of the autumn countryside, the nostalgia of Thanksgiving and Christmas, and to emphasize the billions this country was sending abroad to feed the hungry of other lands.

John never heard this plea. Under the strict discipline of the camp at Panmunjom, all of the twenty-one refused to listen to the recordings from their families and friends.

Like the rest, John Dunn had never been interested in politics and had no personal contact with Communism before he was captured.

"I don't think I ever heard him use the word," said Dr. Baker, who thought that more awareness might have helped.

"Perhaps if youngsters knew something of the insidious and subtle methods of Communism, knew about the sugar coating on the pill, that would have helped. I also believe that our school systems put too little emphasis on American history. I am appalled at the lack of knowledge of their own country displayed by most young people. Not just geography, but roots and traditions."

Dr. Baker felt that no one who had not been through what "John went through" can tell how he would have reacted. "You just don't know because you don't know what the circumstances were."

One of his high school teachers thought John would be particularly vulnerable to Communist peace propaganda.

"He was a mild-mannered boy, who took the ills of others personally. He wanted to be happy and he wanted everybody else to be happy too. He didn't have the kind of mind to see through the relationships between Communism and his wish to see everybody happy.

"He was not a strong boy physically. He would be able to take little physical torture or hardship. Once he was backed in a corner he wouldn't know how to turn around and get out of it. He would not be able to summon up the physical and moral courage to say, 'I've had enough of this.'"

Before the twenty-one left for China, John made a statement to correspondents:

"Our concerted stand will make people realize why we stay here. By doing so, we are putting the anti-peace policies, as contrasted to our own peace policies, in a bright light, for the people to see and examine."

Mrs. William R. Dunn read the statement and looked at the picture of her son. She buried her head in her hands and wept. "That doesn't sound like my son," she said.

Her son would hardly recognize his mother if he returned

today. She looks as emaciated as if she too has been in prison camp. His father's face has taken on sad, grim lines.

After that the family had its phone number changed and moved to a secret address "to get away from all the people who kept asking us what kind of a boy John was that he joined the Communists."

Mrs. Dunn wrote her own story of her son's life for the New York *Herald Tribune*'s *This Week* magazine (June 6, 1954, with June and Jhan Robbins).

"Maybe we spoiled him," Mrs. Dunn wrote, "I don't know. You know how it is with the first one. Jack was always a good child. The only mischief I ever remember him getting into was when he ate a whole tube of toothpaste and broke out in terrible hives."

His younger brother was such a handful that "I was glad when Barbara turned out to be a girl," Mrs. Dunn added.

When they moved to Baltimore the year Jack was thirteen, Mrs. Dunn was "lonely" and decided to go to work too.

"It turned out all right," she said. "Jack was a big help. He could always tell when I was tired. He would push me away from the sink and take over."

Like the other mothers, Mrs. Dunn pondered long and in vain, seeking to answer the incessant question of how this could have happened to her son.

"Could it be that Jack is mentally ill? Maybe his headaches started again and they worked on him when he was in that condition. . . . Maybe he has an incurable disease. . . . Jack wouldn't want to be a burden to us. Maybe they threatened his family . . . or maybe they sold him a bill of goods that Communism is going to help humanity. . . . I guess I'll never see my boy again. If they have really converted him to Communism it would be better if they buried him."

That was in contrast to what she had said that last day, when he left for China with the others.

"Even now," she said then, through her tears, "even now, I'd be glad to have him back—in the face of courtmartial and dishonorable discharge. My son!"

Cpl. Andrew Fortuna

of Detroit, Mich.

born March 20, 1926

Bronze Star with Oak Leaf Cluster

re-enlisted May 12, 1948

1st Cavalry

captured November 27, 1951

Catholic

2 years high school

average I.Q.

The Army Reported:

According to returned prisoners of war, Fortuna was paid by the Chinese to write articles some of which were published in the camp newspaper. He voluntarily joined a Communist study group and attempted to influence other prisoners. He was chosen by the Communists as a public address system announcer because of his reliability.

H<small>IS MOTHER HAD DISAPPEARED</small> into the shadows of Detroit's Skid Row. His half-brother was serving a prison term. His stepfather was dead, but the rift between them could not have been healed anyway. He and his Japanese wife had called it quits after their infant son had died of polio.

Andrew Fortuna, Jr., was twenty-seven and on his third enlistment in the army when he turned his back on his country. His heroism under fire had been recognized by the Bronze Star and Oak Leaf Cluster, won on the Korean battlefields. A less socially acceptable kind of courage had been recognized by a courtmartial for "misappropriating a truck."

Few who met this big, husky blond with the open-faced grin and the twinkling blue eyes would guess that tragedy had stalked him from his earliest days.

Andrew was born Ray Kraft in a small Ohio town in 1926. His mother came to Detroit when he was four and the depression was on, looking for work, a place to live, some future for her fatherless boy. She met Andrew Fortuna, an immigrant laborer. He married her, adopted the boy and gave him his name. The Fortunas had two children of their own, Donald and Viola. But the marriage was never a happy one.

The bickering and quarreling was so extreme that Andrew used to "stay out in the streets nights to keep from going home."

Interviewed in Detroit while he was awaiting a decision

that sent him back to serve out a sentence with a Florida chain gang, his half-brother Donald said of Andrew: "He was the same as thousands of kids his age; he never had much at home. Nothing but trouble in our family. Seems like it should get better but it don't."

Mrs. Fortuna became a problem drinker and used to disappear from home for days at a time. Welfare assistance was needed constantly by the family, for clothes, food and medical care.

At school Andrew got only passing grades though his teachers felt he could have done better. A distinct extrovert, he made himself and his presence known wherever he was, even if it involved a fight. On the street and in the classroom he was continually involved in such struggles.

Yet, compared to his younger brother, he was quiet and restrained. Donald got in trouble first for "ditching" school. Next he was caught shoplifting. Then came robbery. Andrew resented the notoriety brought on the family by Donald's brushes with the police.

I talked to officers at the police station in Lincoln Park, a suburb of Detroit where the family lived. They remember both boys well and recalled a time when Donald evaded them after stealing a gun and $1,000. They went to Andrew and said:

"Now, we know he's got a gun and you can be sure we're not going to let any cops get killed taking him. So if you want to help him, you'll get him to come in and give himself up."

"Go ahead and shoot the S.O.B.," said Andrew bitterly. "He's no good anyway."

Later when Andrew went to the Lincoln Park station to get a statement that he had no police record to turn in with his enlistment papers, an officer who didn't know him got out the Fortuna file and whistled at its length. Andy looked at it and pointed out that it was his brother's, not his.

"I'll be glad to get out of this damn town," he said. "Everybody knows the Fortuna name too damn well."

The police remembered Andrew as a quiet boy. Their contact with him was always on account of his brother. He never got into trouble, and his brother was always in trouble. But they assessed him as "the kind of boy who didn't care anything about anything or anybody."

Andrew was only fifteen the first time he enlisted in the army. Big for his age, he passed as eighteen. School authorities, tracing him as a truant, discovered he was in the army. They called in his mother. She wasn't sure that the army wasn't the best place for him despite his age. She thought maybe they could handle him better than she could. He was discharged, then, however, only to go back shortly after his eighteenth birthday and serve in the Rhineland and Central European campaigns.

Mustered out in November of 1945, Andrew tried civilian life for two and a half years before re-enlisting. He worked as a laborer on construction jobs and earned good pay and the respect of his employers. Now that he had money in his pockets, Andrew was beginning to drink. His quarrels with his stepfather became more serious. On May 12, 1948, he enlisted for the third time.

In November, 1949, he was convicted by a courtmartial "for misappropriating a truck" and was fined $47.28 a month for six months. He went to Japan with the 1st Cavalry Division and landed with his regiment in Korea in July of 1950, when the war was but a few weeks old. He fought through all the engagements of the struggle up and down the peninsula, surviving the defeats which resulted in the capture of most of the others of the twenty-one. He was awarded the Bronze Star January 22, 1951, for endangering his life to take an enemy position. He was awarded the Oak Leaf Cluster May 20, 1951, for leading a platoon in an attack on an enemy hill and for killing twenty-five of the enemy.

He was captured, ironically enough, the day after the twenty-day peace negotiation "lull" started on November 27, 1951, a year later than most of the twenty-one.

Although the army listed him as a public address system announcer for the Reds, chosen because of his "reliability," those who knew him in camp say that he was "reactionary" during most of his two and a half years in prison camp.

One fellow prisoner of war said he knew Andy "hadn't fallen for that stuff, because we used to discuss it together."

And William Allen, a returned prisoner of war who lived a few blocks from Fortuna's home in Lincoln Park but had known him only in prison camp, was sure he wasn't a progressive during the period they were in the same camp.

"He was a good boy, who didn't even pal around with the progressives when I knew him," Allen told me. "I got moved to another camp. We were the first to be sent down to Panmunjom. On our way we stopped at his camp and I asked if Andy was around. They told me he was up the road working."

Allen thought that better than 10 per cent of the prisoners had become progressives—"those that were afraid and a lot of the sick and wounded."

It was pretty tough in camp, he said, particularly the first year.

"More than 1,600 died in two and a half months," he said. "We didn't have any clothes or food or anything. We could always tell when the peace talks were going good. Then we would get something to eat. When they were going bad, they'd clamp down on us."

Shortly after his name was listed as one of the group who

would refuse to be repatriated, Joseph Hainline of Detroit's station WJR did a documentary recording on Andrew Fortuna. Andrew's brother Donald was still accessible and so was one of his friends who has since disappeared.

That was Bob Napolitana, who had been his closest friend for years. In the recording Napolitana said that "his dad didn't like the way Andy was spending his own pay, so Andy would get drunk before he got home, so one day his dad decided that was just enough and he kicked Andy out and Andy re-enlisted a short time later."

Napolitana got a letter from Andrew early in 1953.

"I don't think you'll hardly know me when I return home in the future," he wrote, "for I have broke myself from the bottle while I was in Japan. While I was in Japan I was married to a Japanese girl for two years. We had a little baby boy, but he died of the polio. I think that's the real thing that straightened me out. After the kid died, we come to a mutual understanding and we called it quits.

"I have hopes of buying me a new car when I get out of here but I don't know for sure. I guess you know how my family have split up since my dad died. I haven't made up my mind whether to get it together again or be a bachelor."

Donald, on the same program, made a plea for understanding, not just for Andrew but for the whole group:

"Don't condemn my brother or the other fellows. Pity them. Get them back home where they belong. Either that two and a half years in prison camp has affected him mentally or those men actually believe that what they are doing is right."

Walter Gibson, principal of the Lafayette School (which Andrew attended last, leaving in the eighth grade), told of how much Andrew wanted to make friends and be recognized in his classroom.

"I imagine that his fighting and his trouble-making were attempts to gain recognition with his classmates so he would be considered one of them. Perhaps he didn't make it with his classmates. . . . His home life was very unpleasant. His problem started from the fact that he needed love and affection he should have had at home so that he would fit in the group here with his classmates."

Mrs. Fortuna's absence from home had become permanent by the time her husband died of cancer in 1951. A bartender who knew her said:

"I didn't know whether she worked or not. I know she was always worried about her son in service and she thought he was dead as she had read in the papers that he was unaccounted for."

Except for the last one, none of Andrew's letters home contained the usual Communist line which filled even the letters of many boys who came back. That last one was written in May of 1953 to his brother Donald.

"There are a lot of things the American people ought to know about what's going on here. We are going to tell them. Only big business is benefitting from this war. All the people want peace."

Claude Batchelor made a recording for Joseph Hainline of WJR before he was taken into custody. He had this to say about Fortuna:

"I think the way the Communists managed to influence him was to work on his lower class background. He had somewhat of a struggle maybe, going through life, and the Communists always like to preach those things to you. . . . From the way Andrew talked, I'm convinced he didn't have any selfish gains in mind. He was just mixed up."

At any rate, Andrew stayed with the twenty-one. Just before he left for China he made the usual statement for correspondents:

"Like the rest of the men, my main reason for staying behind is to fight for peace. But perhaps I understand even a little better how important world peace is. I fought in World War II against the Fascists. I come back to find Fascists in my own country in the form of McCarthy and men of his caliber. I don't want to go back to that but I will as soon as the people of the United States get rid of the McCarthys and the Veldes."

One day in the spring of 1954 after Andy had gone into the interior of China, Mrs. Fortuna collapsed and died in a Michigan Avenue bar. "Acute alcoholism" was given as the reason for her death.

There has been no word from her son since the Iron Curtain closed on him.

Pvt. James G. Veneris

of Vandergrift, Pa.

born March 27, 1922

re-enlisted 1950

2nd Division

captured December 1, 1951

Greek Catholic

high school grad

above average I.Q.

The Army Reported:

According to returned prisoners of war, Veneris' collaboration included giving lectures on Communism, leading study groups, signing and circulating petitions, trying to influence his fellow prisoners to accept Communism and acting as liaison man and librarian at his camp.

"Y<small>AH</small>! Y<small>AH</small>! Dirty imperialists!"

The stocky, dark-haired American soldier in the Chinese padded blue uniform, spit the words out venomously and jumped up and down in his rage at the U.N. representatives that had approached the barricades of the neutral compound at Panmunjom.

This was Jimmie Veneris of Vandergrift, Pa., known as "the Greek" all up and down the prison camps run by the so-called Chinese People's Volunteers.

Oldest of the twenty-one—he is thirty-three—Veneris is not Greek, but was born in the United States, though both his parents were born in Greece and neither ever learned to speak English. All his life he wanted to be accepted as an American. He refused to learn more than a minimum of Greek and he broke out of the Greek clique in his home town to pal with boys whose national origins were less defined. But he was still "the Greek" even in prison camp.

I talked to his mother out in Hawthorne, Calif., a suburb of Los Angeles, where all the family but Jimmie had moved after World War I. His sister Anastasia acted as interpreter. His father, George J. Veneris, had died of cancer a few weeks earlier, his death hastened, it was said, by his sorrow over his son's decision.

"I don't know what to say or what to think," Mrs. Veneris told me. "He must have been under terrible pressure to come to believe these things." Her strong face was gaunt with pain. "I pray every night and every day."

"He always hated Communists," Anastasia added on her own. "He always said that people who were Communists should go back and live in Russia. . . ." She broke off suddenly, remembering that her brother was, in a way, under his own sentence.

His family had received odd letters, like so many others, criticizing his country for "germ warfare" and "for continuing this war and making the peoples of the world suffer," but his last letter had spoken of his eagerness to be home by Christmas.

His mother thought perhaps he had been brought up too strictly although he was never slapped or spanked—"His father hollered at him when he didn't do what he was supposed to."

His family thought Jimmie friendly and cooperative, quiet and confident but occasionally stubborn and somewhat moody.

While I was talking with them the mailman came with a thin flat package. It was the tape recording that Mr. and Mrs. Veneris had made in the hope that their son would hear it and come back home to them. With it was a letter telling them that as far as the army knew he had not heard it—at any rate he hadn't come home.

In Vandergrift, a steel mill town less than an hour's drive from Pittsburgh, the shock was just as great. Ralph W. McIntyre, burgess of the town, called Jimmie one of the best-liked young men in town. Others spoke of how much he had appreciated being an American, how proud he was of his country.

Unlike most of the twenty-one, he had many friends in all walks of life, growing up. He had a high-average I.Q. and had the best school record of any of the group, getting mostly B's with a few C's. He had to work after school—he ushered at a movie house—so athletics were out of the question, but he had participated to some extent in the social activities of his classmates. He belonged to the Stamp Club and he had been in the stage crew of the Christmas play. He always had a girl for the school dance. He was a good talker—pick a subject and he knew something about it—he read a lot on his own, especially in psychology and psychiatry.

But there were some who saw the hopes and ambitions, the frustrations and resentments below the surface.

Vandergrift is a charming town that climbs the hills steeply from the river where the railroad station, mill and shopping center are located. It is a town without a slum—or if it has one it is the narrow street where Jimmie Veneris lived. It is also a town singularly free from race or national prejudices; the Greek element, however, tends to keep to itself. His father had a laborer's job and Jimmie minded that.

"We felt in a way," one of his teachers said, "that he grew up without parents because, with the language barrier, there was so little communication between him and them."

He wanted desperately to get ahead, another teacher told me, but he wanted to do it quickly; he wanted to hit the top of the ladder without touching the other rungs. And he felt that other people "didn't appreciate what he had to offer."

This was confirmed by a leading member of the Greek community whom he respected and to whom he turned when he needed help.

"He was always up in the clouds, always reading," he said. "He wanted to be a big shot, but he wasn't much in love with work. He wanted easy work, something not too hard. But he was good-natured and polite, always considerate. He borrowed money from me from time to time but he always paid it back. He did not get along with his father, and his mother couldn't help him understand because she couldn't talk English and he couldn't talk Greek."

That he should have deserted his country was too hard to believe—"He was as American as American can be."

"I had to laugh," he added, "when the Bishop of New York sent him this long letter in Greek about Spartan patriotism in the great days of Greece, and I thought, That boy will get nothing out of that. So we wrote him a letter from Vandergrift where he grew up and had his friends. People who went to school with him and all the people that he knew signed it. I don't know, though, that he ever got it."

Jimmie Veneris' last year in high school was colored as it was for the rest of his classmates by the World War II draft and the impending threat of war. He graduated in June of 1940 and was in the army by August—to stay for five years and take part in the New Guinea campaign.

When he was discharged he got a job at U. S. Steel, not that quick hop up the ladder he had hoped for but a laborer's job as a stocker's helper, sweeping and cleaning up.

"It wasn't the kind of job that a boy of his intelligence would find much in," William Atkinson, personnel director at the plant, said, "but at that particular period there wasn't much chance for advancement. We were cutting down operations. It was a slack period."

Jimmie got laid off and worked at various jobs, as an usher, as he had earlier after school; as a waiter in a restaurant. His family moved to California but he refused to go with them.

Finally, in September of 1950, he re-enlisted. The date is important because the Korean fighting had already started. Veneris was one of the few among the twenty-one who went into the army knowing there was a war on and he might get into it.

A month after he went in, Veneris was en route to the front, as a badly needed replacement for the mauled 2nd Division. He survived the Chinese offensive at the end of November that pushed United Nations troops pellmell back from the Yalu River, and was captured a year later on December 1, 1951, during the "quiet" period when peace negotiations seemed certain of success. Though he was reported to have fallen for the Communist line early, he was never accused of being an informer.

I sat across the counter from Jack Jarackas in the Sweetland Chocolate Shoppe in Vandergrift and waited for the noon rush to let up. Between whipping up a milk shake and fixing a bacon and tomato sandwich, Jarackas talked to me about his good friend, Jimmie Veneris.

"I can't make it out," he said. "He just wasn't the type. Why, he was crazy about the army. Even when he was out of it he talked like an army man, he even walked like an army man. And he wrote me from camp he was going to make the army his career.

"Sure, he wasn't like the rest of us. He had a lot of ideas. He wanted to be on the first spaceship to Mars. And he could talk about psychology and biology and things like that with experts and hold his own. He was kind of somber except when he had a load on and then he was the happiest guy in the world; that's the only time he would dance. Sometimes he'd go along with us and other times he just wouldn't show up; he'd disappear. When he was working at the mill he would sneak up back alleys on his way home from work because he didn't want anybody to see him in his dirty work clothes. He was the cleanest guy I ever knew."

The Harding family, who have a big rambling house on

225—

one of Vandergrift's pleasant tree-shaded avenues, were puzzled too. Jimmie had spent many hours in that house, making it almost a second home, and he and Allen Harding were buddies.

From prison camp he wrote them a letter:

It sure is a funny war. I hear coffee is about ninety cents a pound back there and when I think of coffee it reminds me of the Harding family. I wish I had a dollar for every cup I have drank back at your place; I guess I could buy myself a new Buick car. I also miss the good old bull sessions we used to have. I'll be back some day and we can all converse again.

And that sounded like him, but then there was this:

Ever since our capture we have been treated good under the guidance of the CPV (Chinese People's Volunteers). They have a policy called the lenient treatment. I have never even been sworn at by these people.

Even with letters like that, no one in Vandergrift or in Hawthorne where his folks now live was prepared to have Jimmie Veneris become one of the twenty-one or to make the statement that he made the day the group left for China:

"The guys who did go back as sick and wounded or in repatriation exchange and who are interested in world peace— they were declared misfits and put into mental wards at Valley Forge. (Some of the early returned prisoners of war were interviewed there before their discharge.) It was a very unjust treatment for men whose main aim in life was to help mankind by fighting for peace. I love my country, my people, my parents. I will return when peace is established and McCarthy and clique are abolished."

—226

Outwitting the Brainwashers

THE STORY OF how the Chinese Reds subjugated the twenty-one American prisoners of war to the point where they refused to come home is a horror story without relief, with the victims writing their own death warrants and supplying the weapons for their own destruction.

It is a revelation of how the compassionate techniques of modern psychiatry are perverted to the cold business of changing an individual into a utility, of how group loyalty is twisted into group tyranny, surveillance and coercion; of how invasion of privacy ends inevitably in the blanking out of free will and finally of personality itself.

No one reading the unhappy life stories of the twenty-one—stories of broken homes, poverty, brutal treatment, serious emotional problems and scanty education—could fail to see how vulnerable they were, how pitifully ill-equipped to withstand the psychological warfare the Reds waged against them.

Does this mean then that the kid down the street would be safe? Hardly. Millions of American boys are growing up under circumstances that would make them just as vulnerable, were they exposed in the same way as were the twenty-one.

And if the underprivileged and the weak, the rejected and the sinned against, are lambs for the Communist slaughter of innocence, that is not the whole story.

Beyond that, no one, however stalwart, however secure,

however ideal his background—only that paragon without a flaw, without a secret, without a hidden hurt—could withstand the full force of the cruelly corroding methods the Communists use, unless armed with the only successful defense, knowledge of what those methods are and how they achieve their ends.

We cannot just shed a tear for the twenty-one and go on to breathe a sigh of satisfaction that after all there were only twenty-one. There could have been more. There were more who volunteered. There were at least four hundred who became progressives, collaborating with the Chinese to the extent of taking an active part in their propaganda campaign, attempting to win others over to the line and even informing on their hutmates.

Fortunately, the Communists were not able to bring their full force to bear at every point; fortunately they were not infallible and made some mistakes; and finally, time was against them when they belatedly decided, forty days before the armistice, to parry the effect of the twenty-three thousand prisoners of war on their side who refused to return home.

This meant that they could only develop a token force to keep back and had to pick those whom their methods would soften up most quickly. That is why it is these particular twenty-one who will never come home.

Some of the most likely progressives had already been sent back to do a propaganda job in the United States, "ringers" in the limited exchange of wounded prisoners in April of 1953 ("Operation Little Switch") which took place before the Communists decided how to parry the fact that thousands of their own prisoners of war would refuse repatriation.

Those who remained, whether progressives or not, had been through the weakening torture, the despair and uncertainty of almost three years of prison life. They had suffered from privation and lack of privacy; they had been subjected to blaring, relentless propaganda, day in and day out, and the further psychological effects of little or no word from home.

The Communists had to have leaders for the group and these were carefully selected from among those who had already been worked over. For the rest, in their scheme of things, it was necessary only that they be controllable—sheep —or men who had broken down under the stresses of prison life and were for that reason malleable.

So far as possible the Communists chose the twenty-one from what they termed the peasant and the beggar class: poor marginal farm dwellers and town-bred relief clients. Only a few with leadership qualities were needed. For this they chose: Corden, the proud New Englander with the high I.Q. who had never recovered from the beatings of his childhood; Sullivan, the Negro athletic champion with the unhappy history; and Tenneson, the Minnesota boy who had lived around and whose innately bright mind had never found a channel.

Then they sat them down and told them to write the stories of their lives. And did not tell them why. They wrote a page, maybe a page and a half. Do it over again, they were told; write more; and over again, and more, until they had written perhaps fifty pages.

They were not told—they did not know—that everything they said would be used against them. And in those pages they revealed themselves. They could not help it. No matter how masked with verbiage, they stood revealed: their hates and their loves, their shames and their misplaced hopes, their dreams and their weaknesses.

To be a prisoner means to lead one's life in public. Now with the Communists' knowledge of their inner thoughts and feelings, they were stripped of all privacy. Through their detailed knowledge of their past lives, gleaned from the stories they had themselves written, the Communists had the clues to each man's personality and the means to eliminate his individuality. They could repress or encourage the elements they wanted.

They reconstructed a man's life story and evaluated it in their own terms, made him see it as they saw it, in a calculated inversion of the technique a psychiatrist uses to help a patient gain greater insight and understanding of his past.

They could probe old wounds and make them flare up again. When a cause of resentment showed up in the victim's story, they could lead him by easy stages up to the point where they could persuade him that it was the system that was at fault.

To those who showed that they felt rejected they would give sympathy and attention.

"You see that we don't reject you. It's the system—American imperialism—not you, that is wrong."

For one, they might bring up incidents in his past which could be used to make a prisoner squirm and then convince him that it would be embarrassing, perhaps even dangerous, for him to go home.

The same technique was used in connection with incidents that happened at camp, specifically the signatures they had managed to corral from almost everyone on peace petitions. They would bring a candidate in and show him the "fine print" he hadn't bothered to read when he signed it, or even a completely different document with his signature clipped and pasted on.

"Of course you can't go home after signing this," they would point out, ever so gently.

It was even easier with those they had led into informing

on their prison mates. It wasn't hard to convince Billy Cowart, for instance, that he had no friends among the Americans—only among the Chinese; or that he had gone so far he couldn't come back.

Nor was it difficult to play on Richard Tenneson's feelings that he'd never had a square deal. Or to show Richard Corden, whom they installed as leader, that his proud abilities had been consistently ignored all his life until he got to prison camp.

They got to LaRance Sullivan, the Negro from Santa Barbara, through his tortured mixture of love and shame for his unfortunate mother.

"It was the system that was wrong, not your mother. In our culture she is a heroine; in America she was put in jail for faults that were not hers but the system's."

With Belgian-born Albert Belhomme, in many ways the most knowledgeable of the group, it was still possible to use his hopes for a brave new world and the hatred of Hitlerism which he had gained during his years under Nazi occupation.

Since he had lived in America but a short time and it had happened to him once before it was not hard to convince him that the United States was now dominated by a home-grown variety of Nazism.

For Morris Wills, his marriage to a Chinese nurse, the daughter of a Communist general, was the jumping-off point.

To woo Otho Bell, letters from his wife could be withheld or manipulated to make it appear that she had deserted him.

With Veneris, his nickname, "the Greek," was the tool to persuade him that he had never been truly accepted by his fellow Americans.

With Andrew Fortuna, the touchstones were many: his difficulties with his stepfather; his mother's inadequacies; his brushes with the police over his brother's criminal career.

It took no genius to persuade Elbert Douglas that only the Chinese had any interest in him. And so it went, on down the line.

But this was only the beginning. To get them to agree not to go home was one thing; to assure that they could be counted on not to waver in that decision was of prime importance.

To accomplish this the Chinese brought into play techniques that sound like a chapter out of George Orwell's *1984*. These consisted of group and self-criticism; in the degree they were used on the American prisoners of war, they are a peculiarly Chinese contribution to Communist methods.

The chosen twenty-three were brought together as a group; they studied together, played together, worked together, ate together, slept together—under control.

Every day they had a session of "group criticism."

"What was Webb doing at three o'clock this morning, talking to outsider John Doe?"

Webb was just exchanging pleasantries with the outsider, but he had to explain himself. The next time he has such an encounter he will tell on himself first, for fear someone else saw him. The sense of surveillance, of eyes on him at all times becomes complete. He does not even dare think outside the pattern for fear it might show.

This technique was refined to an even further degree when the group got to the compound at Panmunjom. No letter or message came into or went out of the compound that wasn't read aloud to the whole group.

No decision was made by any man on his own. No man was allowed to talk to any outsider on his own. The letters written to Wilson's sister and Tenneson's mother when she came to Tokyo were group compositions.

The Communists had selected the twenty-three on the

basis of "reliability" rather than their adherence to Communist precepts. Under the Communist system you use the individual where you can—as a utility. He doesn't have to be a Communist to be used. In order to be considered reliable he has only to be placed in a niche and be willing to stay there.

They were wrong about the reliability of two of the men: Batchelor and Dickenson. They could have been wrong about some of the others and they knew it. That's why the group discipline had to be so strong at camp and be augmented by the fact that 325 South Korean non-repatriates surrounded them in the compound.

Dickenson's "escape" was an ironic accident. LaRance Sullivan, whom the Chinese had worked on until they were sure of his reliability, was planted in the hospital outside the compound. He was suffering from tuberculosis, but that wasn't the reason he was in the hospital. He was there as the group agent to keep under control any of the others who might be taken ill.

What happened with Dickenson had not been foreseen or blueprinted. He developed a throbbing toothache at two in the morning. His bunk mates refused to wake up and give him any sympathy. He walked the court, up and down, and up and down. Finally he appealed to an Indian guard, who could not speak English but at least gathered the prisoner of war was in pain and took him to the hospital. Sullivan was asleep. The Indian doctor who came to treat him could speak English.

"Why don't you want to go home?" the doctor said.

Dickenson's toothache seemed to have washed out the automatic responses the Communists had taught him.

"I do want to go home," he said. The door to freedom that opened for him then may prove instead to be a door to federal prison, if the ten-year sentence he has been given is upheld on appeal.

Claude Batchelor was the second—and the last—to come out. He too is under sentence now: twenty years. Letters from his Japanese wife were given credit for making him change his mind. But his demotion as leader of the group in favor of Corden may have interrupted the patterns the Communists had laid down in his mind sufficiently to allow himself to pull free.

"You see," he wrote to Jewell Bell, wife of one of the twenty-one who stayed, "I exerted a lot of influence over those fellows. In every election they held I got a unanimous vote from everyone. They looked to me for guidance in Marxist philosophy until I became convinced that what I was doing was wrong."

Batchelor tried to explain to Mrs. Bell what happened to the prisoners of war during their imprisonment.

"You see he (Bell) like myself," Batchelor wrote, "was one of those prisoners of war who wanting to do good for the American people fell for a bit of the Communist propaganda and became what was known as progressives. But other G.I.'s started labeling them rats, informers, traitors, etc. when actually they were under the impression that what they were doing was right.

"When you consider the fact that we prisoners of war never heard one controversial word concerning the Communists in over three years of captivity whereas we had nothing but Communism dinned into our minds for over three years, it is no wonder that hundreds of prisoners of war wanting to be good Americans, believed what the Communists told them, and ruined themselves, thinking they were doing a heroic thing.

"Myself I can never be the same again, thinking how I

was deceived. I can only thank God I found out in time. Yet, I shall always feel bad because I failed in my efforts to get others to follow me. . . .

"I saw several young American boys who either died or were killed in the Korean conflict. I almost got killed myself. It made one's blood boil at the terrible destruction of innocent lives. But instead of directing my hate where it belonged to the people that caused these men to die, I directed it to the men who sent them eight thousand miles away to be killed. I considered the Korean war to be useless. I blamed not the Communists for killing these men, but the American government for sending them to die.

"Three years' experience has given me an education I shall never forget. I know now beyond all doubt that the Korean war was by no means useless as many Americans today think. I know we owe a lot to the men in government to have the foresight to send our troops to Korea before the Communists had a chance to take over the Philippines, Japan and eventually the United States."

Commenting on the future of the twenty-one, Batchelor wrote:

"I believe the Chinese will send them to school like they promised. But a Communist school is nothing like our system of free education. They will have nothing but Communism to read in magazines, novels, newspapers and to see in the movies. They will not be able to forget it for one moment. In short, they will read, eat, sleep and play Communism until there is nothing else left in their distorted minds' pictures. In a few years as former Americans they will point to America with a certain amount of authority in Communist countries and say terrible things about their homeland."

The courtmartial actions taken against Dickenson and Batchelor bring up an important point. Although none of the twenty-three recalcitrant prisoners of war were promised forgiveness for any crimes they committed in prison camp, they were assured that if they changed their minds and came home, the fact that they had temporarily been persuaded to refuse repatriation would not be held against them.

Technically, that promise has been kept. They have been sentenced only for offenses committed in prison camp. But since many—perhaps hundreds—of other prisoners of war who committed similar offenses have not been brought to trial, it seems obvious that they were prosecuted chiefly because of their connection with the group.

It is notable, too, that up to this writing the few officers put on trial for collaborating with the enemy and informing on fellow prisoners have been usually acquitted—in one case sentenced merely to "involuntary discharge," the officer corps euphemism for what would be dishonorable discharge for an enlisted man.

All during the three-month period allowed by the armistice for "explanations" by their own countrymen, the group refused to listen to our official explainers. They also censored letters from family and friends; the pathetic recordings that each home circle made to appeal to their boy were not allowed inside the compound. Only at the end, when the twenty-one were about to leave for China and the final days of grace were over, were newspaper correspondents permitted to speak to them. And then they all parroted the same sentiments.

For these twenty-one, hope is gone. From the Communist point of view they are "expendable utilities," according to Joseph D. Lohman, Chicago University sociologist who acted as consultant to the U.N. Repatriation Command in Korea.

"With all their shortcomings—these were plentiful and used by the Communists in establishing their control—they were caught in the seamless web of Communist intrigue, conspiracy, and group methods of control and indoctrination," Lohman says, but he thinks there is an answer for the future.

"If and when the unrelenting and coercive group methods of the Communists are exposed and made widely known, they become powerless and ineffective. Communism must be recognized for what it is, a diabolical power system. A major answer to the Communist threat is to make clear to those who may be exposed to its methods, the nature of those methods and the way in which they are designed to break an individual through the destruction of his privacy and an all-embracing system of collective coercion."

Certainly American prisoners of war were not prepared sufficiently for the psychological strains they were to bear. The six hours of classes in psychological warfare and Communism scheduled for every G.I. are obviously ineffective; most prisoners of war do not recall ever hearing anything about Communism in their army training.

Our soldiers were never given any understanding of the reasons why they were fighting in Korea. They had no answers for the Communist gibes.

Nor did their schools give them any rounded idea of what Communism is or what it stands for. For the twenty-one, as for most of the prisoners of war that did return, Communism was a dirty word, a faceless menace.

Most educators I talked to believe that Communism should be a subject for instruction in the schools; that the "climate" of our times prevents it; that they are further hindered by having few teachers who themselves know enough about it to teach.

Because of their ignorance that Communism is sometimes, if only verbally, "on the side of the angels," these twenty-one, with their religious upbringing, were astounded to hear the Chinese express Biblical sentiments about the "brotherhood of man" and "peace on earth." It made it easy for the Chinese to convince many that the lies were on their own side rather than on the Communist side.

In this context it is particularly interesting that the Negroes, no better educated than their white comrades in arms, were much more sophisticated on the subject of Communism —"A lot of our boys had been worked over by them back home."

The army's replacement system, together with its lack of emphasis on pride of outfit for the lowly infantryman, can take some share of the blame. Charles Loutitt, of Monongahela, Pa., who won the Bronze Star for his heroism in prison camp, belonged to the 187th Regiment—airborne—and he was proud of it. He and nine others from his outfit formed a phalanx so solid against Communist efforts to corrupt them that they had to be broken up and separated.

The problem presented by the personality weaknesses of the twenty-one prisoners of war the Communists caught is more diverse. Educators in every section of the country pointed out that the problems of the slow learner, the emotionally disturbed child, the withdrawn child are widespread. These twenty-one do not represent isolated cases but represent millions who grow up hurt and undereducated.

As of now, few communities are equipped to cope with a problem which must be met on three levels: the economic, the educational and the psychological.

In Akron a start has been made in one phase. The Miller Occupational School, which Rush attended, deals with the problem of the slow learners, a problem which has taken on increased importance with the comparatively recent laws compelling truly universal education in this country.

Formerly, students who did not do well in school could drop out and find a niche for themselves. Now, laws prevent children from leaving school before they are sixteen; and fewer and fewer jobs of any kind are open to the illiterate. The slow learner who does not get special attention gets no more education, even when he is passed up from grade to grade, than if he had dropped out; he is only subjected to the scorn of his brighter classmates and leaves school with the added burden of a consciousness of his own "stupidity" and a feeling of being an outsider.

In addition, the impact of the slow learner on the general classroom has slowed the progress of the particularly gifted student, even dulled the wits of the bright boy and led him into habits that may mean he will never fulfill his own promise.

The problem of the country school boy transferring to a consolidated town high school cropped up in several of the life stories. Principals are aware of the difficulty of integrating the rural children with the town children. And they are aware of the further problem of the farm child whose parents often are impatient with the time their child "wastes" in school. Neither problem has yet been solved.

The emotionally disturbed child, either on the increase or more readily recognized than formerly, adds to the general problem of education.

Only in Santa Barbara, LaRance Sullivan's home town, of all I visited, has a beginning been made in considering the whole problem of the child and his environment, in recognizing that every child who is not helped means a new generation of children who will need further help.

Dr. Charlotte D. Elmott, director of child guidance in Santa Barbara, believes strongly that the community's program must be concerned with "the least of these" if "we are to bring up citizens strong enough to defend American democracy."

"We have made considerable gains in our community since the war," she said, "and have added a mental hygiene clinic and have much better use of psychiatric consultancy." However, the growth of the city and the increase of the child population "means that many social agencies must limit their services to children whose problems are already clearly defined, thus taking their attention from preventive work with very little children."

What about patriotism? Did the twenty-one lack a feeling of love and loyalty for their country? Their schools taught them to salute the flag and to sing "The Star-Spangled Banner." It is true that most of them entered the army for other than patriotic reasons. Only three enlisted after the beginning of the Korean fighting. Only one enlisted with the express desire to fight for his country. This was Tenneson who said "even if I should win the Congressional Medal of Honor it would not be enough to do for my country!" Yet, he was as easy a prey for the Communists as any of the twenty-one.

Patriotism is not easy to pin down. But it seems clear that love of country must be based on love of home and community first of all. Few of these twenty-one had much reason to love their home or their community. Few had ever had a stable home—or anything stable in their lives to which they could hold.

There remains the ultimate problem: Every human being has his breaking point, no matter how well prepared for psychological resistance. Starvation and physical torture can so corrupt the mind and the will to resist that no one, however strong, physically, mentally or emotionally to begin with, can be sure he will not break.

Thirty-six American fliers, for instance, signed germ warfare confessions. These were all officers, men with high I.Q.'s, superior education, special training and responsibilities.

Cold, endless repetition, illness, loneliness and systematic degradation, said Marine Col. Frank H. Schwable, brought him to the point where he signed a long and ridiculously detailed confession.

"They say black is white, you say it is not. But you wind up agreeing."

Fellow officers who had not broken testified for him, saying he had undergone more than they had and they could not truly say they could have stood up under the treatment he had received.

Lt. Quinn, who was used to convince prisoners of war that their country was guilty of germ warfare, told a story similar to Schwable's after he returned to freedom.

Solitary confinement, disgusting food, scanty clothing, endless hours of interrogation and repetition led to the eventual wearing away of the will so that "what they told you to say began to have more reality than the truth."

The minds of these men cleared when they hit the air of freedom. This was not so for some of the prisoner of war progressives who returned home.

More spectacular was the "hangover" that Dr. Malcolm Bersohn of New York and Mrs. Adele Austin Rickett of Yonkers, a Fulbright student, displayed when they emerged from Red China in the spring of 1955 after three and a half years in prison under charges of espionage.

Both denounced themselves, in remarkably similar language, for having been "wicked reactionaries" in contrast to the "good" and "peace-loving" Chinese. Of course they were guilty as charged, the two insisted. "No one is arrested in China unless he is guilty."

The suggestion has come from several sources that instead

of limiting our prisoners to the Geneva Convention of giving their name, rank and serial number and then buttoning up their mouths, they be told to admit anything and everything (except military information) that their captors request, and more; that we announce this as a national policy so that nothing they "confess" can be used as a propaganda weapon.

This would give our soldiers not merely a defensive but an offensive weapon against the devious, barbaric and inhuman measures the Communists do not hesitate to use. With it we could sow our own confusion. We would not merely stand and take it; we could hit back.

Whatever decision is made on that score, there are clearly three steps that need to be taken to prevent a recurrence of the tragedy of the twenty-one.

1. Soldiers must be given the ideological weapons they need as well as the guns to fight against the enemy's psychological warfare. They need to know why they are fighting and they need to know the kind of propaganda the enemy will use against them. They also need a greater sense of belonging—pride of outfit.

2. Schools all over the country must be assisted in coping with the problem of the slow learner and the emotionally disturbed child. This is not only for their benefit but for that of the bright children they may hold back and keep from becoming the leaders this country needs.

3. We must not let fear of Communism keep us from being fully informed about it—good points as well as bad—so that future generations are not taken in when they find out that Communists don't beat their grandmothers. The hush-hush, dirty-word attitude toward Communism made these twenty-one a much easier prey for the Chinese Reds than they would ever have been if they had understood how

and why Communism happened and what its aims were and what they have become.

If every man has his breaking point, it still is not necessary to make the process as easy as it was with the twenty-one prisoners of war. Had they had any sophistication about Communism, the conspiracy which operated so successfully that twenty-one stayed with the Reds might have failed.

Appendix

20 had never heard of Communism except as a dirty word.
20 had no idea what they were fighting for in Korea.
18 grew up in poverty (eight knew real deprivation).
16 came from small towns or rural communities.
17 didn't finish high school.
16 had homes broken by death, divorce or separation.
18 took no part in school activities or sports.
16 were withdrawn, lone wolves (four of these were picked on).
20 were regular army volunteers but only one volunteered to fight.
16 were average or below in I.Q. (five were well below normal).
19 curiously were oldest or only boy in the family.
15 were twenty-one years of age or younger when they were captured; three were seventeen; four were eighteen; five were nineteen.

Two won the Bronze Star for Heroism, five were veterans of World War II; only three were ever in trouble with the army; only three were ever in trouble with the juvenile authorities and that was minor. Two went to college but under relaxed requirements for G.I.'s. Only one came from a big metropolitan city, Detroit. Only one was ever chosen by his classmates for anything. Two were married; one had a child he had never seen.

HOME BACKGROUND—MATERIAL CIRCUMSTANCES

1 of the 21 was well off, better than average.
2 of the 21 were comfortably fixed, about average.
10 of the 21 were poor when boys were growing up, some better off now.
8 of the 21 knew extreme poverty and deprivation.

KIND OF COMMUNITY

6 of the 21   lived in rural communities.
3 of the 21   lived in small towns.
2 of the 21   lived in company towns.
8 of the 21   lived in small cities.
1 of the 21   grew up in metropolitan Detroit.
1 of the 21   grew up in Antwerp, Belgium.

EDUCATIONAL AND INTELLECTUAL BACKGROUND

19 of the 21   were considered undereducated by their teachers no matter what grade they had attained in school; this includes the two "college" boys.
2 of the 21   had satisfactory education.
              Of these:
              One graduated from an American high school with good grades.
              One was European-educated with command of several languages.

SCHOOLING

5 of the 21   didn't go beyond the eighth grade.
13 of the 21 went to high school but didn't finish.
3 of the 21   graduated from high school.
2 of the 21   went to college without finishing high school.

I.Q.

5 of the 21   had better than average I.Q., one extremely high.
              None of these went to college.
11 of the 21 had average or low-average I.Q.
              Two of these went to college.
5 of the 21   had low I.Q.
              Four of these didn't get beyond eighth grade.

FAMILY RELATIONSHIPS

19 of the 21   felt unloved or unwanted by fathers or stepfathers.
2 of the 21   showed signs of emotional maladjustment for undetermined reasons.

BROKEN HOMES

11 of the 21   lost their fathers at an early age, through divorce or death. Three of these also lost their mothers.

2 of the 21   lost their mothers, only, at an early age.

8 of the 21   had both parents, still married, when they went into the army.

THE ELEVEN WHO LOST THEIR FATHERS

8 of the 11   lost fathers through divorce.

3 of the 11   lost fathers through death.

*   *   *   *   *

9 of the 11   mothers remarried; only one boy took stepfather's name. Eight had different names than rest of family.

10 of the 11   had unstable homes, at times lived with relatives, in foster homes, institutions, unsure of where they would go next.

*   *   *   *   *

6 of the 11   were treated with extreme brutality by fathers or stepfathers. In addition, mothers of two of these were problem drinkers.

2 of the 11   got along badly with stepfather.

2 of the 11   had good surface relations with stepfathers but expressed resentment outside home.

1 of the 11   lost stepfather by divorce, too.

THE TWO WHO LOST ONLY THEIR MOTHERS

1 of the 2   had stepmother and resented her.

2 of the 2   were afraid of their fathers.

THE EIGHT WHO HAD BOTH PARENTS

3 of the 8   were afraid of their fathers.

3 of the 8   were estranged from their fathers.

2 of the 8   were seemingly on good terms with their fathers.

*   *   *   *   *

3 of the 8   had unstable homes, fathers who worked or stayed away from home, family moved often.

1 of the 8   had language barrier. Parents could speak no English. He could speak little of their language.

RELATIONSHIP WITH MOTHERS

5 of the 21   lost their mothers when they were young. Three of these also lost their fathers.

5 others	were away from mothers in early childhood; all five had also lost fathers by death or divorce.
2 of the 21	had mothers who were problem drinkers.
4 of the 21	had mothers who worked away from home.
5 of the 21	had mothers who were unusually strict or had high intellectual standards that the boy could not attain.
1 of the 21	could not speak his mother's language; she could not speak English.

POSITION IN FAMILY

19 of the 21	were only or oldest boy.
2 of the 21	were younger sons; both of these lost mothers.

—248

9